Remarkable Learning

Remarkable Learning

A Guidebook for Building Creative and Confident Kids

Daniel J. Evans

BLOOMSBURY ACADEMIC
NEW YORK • LONDON • OXFORD • NEW DELHI • SYDNEY

BLOOMSBURY ACADEMIC
Bloomsbury Publishing Inc, 1359 Broadway, New York, NY 10018, USA
Bloomsbury Publishing Plc, 50 Bedford Square, London, WC1B 3DP, UK
Bloomsbury Publishing Ireland, 29 Earlsfort Terrace, Dublin 2, D02 AY28, Ireland

BLOOMSBURY, BLOOMSBURY ACADEMIC and the Diana logo are trademarks of Bloomsbury Publishing Plc

First published in the United States of America 2026

A catalog record for this book is available from the Library of Congress

ISBN: HB: 979-8-2163-9007-7
PB: 979-8-2163-9008-4
ePDF: 979-8-2164-5069-6
eBook: 979-8-2163-9010-7

Typeset by Newgen KnowledgeWorks Pvt. Ltd., Chennai, India
Printed and bound in the United States of America

For product safety related questions contact productsafety@bloomsbury.com.

To find out more about our authors and books visit www.bloomsbury.com and sign up for our newsletters.

Contents

List of Figures

List of Tables

Preface: Oh, What We Can Do

Without question, the things we seek are within our reach, and don't let anyone tell you differently. No matter what some may say, all children can learn at exceedingly high levels. No matter their backgrounds, home lives, or struggles, they can succeed. Every one of our students can develop academic self-confidence and emotional well-being, all the while gaining a deep understanding of their purpose and place in the world. This unflinching, no-doubt-about-it positivism about what is possible in our schools is not presented as an inspiring vision. It is offered up as fact. It is presented as truth, for it is rooted in sound research, broad observations, and informed practice.

As educators, we know that all children can learn because we have witnessed it countless times without fail. Across our classrooms far and wide, we have seen great teachers cut through the binds of poverty, bureaucracy, and accountability to accomplish unimaginable outcomes that impact children from all walks of life. Across the landscape of a thousand schools in a thousand cities and towns, great teachers are helping children master reading, math, history, science, and many other subjects each day, even in classrooms where students arrive from homes riddled with hardship and trauma.

A master teacher who stares down the critics and brings students to incredible heights is the kind of thing they make movies about. The funny thing is this: It is not all that unusual. There are teachers in every school who make this happen each day, without fanfare. This book honors their work and sacrifice. In fact, this is a call to reinstate our full faith and confidence in our teachers and not our policymakers. This book is not meant to celebrate the exploits of a few magical teachers working in some fairy-tale school setting. On the contrary, it is intended to hold up those who battle on behalf of children every day in every type of school. It is for those who truly believe in the promise of children, and for those who are searching for just the right techniques and pixie dust to know that what works for some teachers can work for all.

In the end, we must study and learn from our best teachers and follow their leads. Nothing fancy. Nothing miraculous. In fact, research and experience have affirmed that any teacher can master and utilize a few surefire, unremarkable moves that can lead to remarkable results. These methods are not groundbreaking, but they are foundational and consequential. In fact, the techniques presented via this text will be familiar to those who have unpacked educational research and studied instructional best practices. Still, reading about high-yield strategies is not the same as putting them into practice. There are some things we can only learn by doing (trial and error), by spending time watching our best teachers in action (observation), and by soaking up their brilliance.

With all due respect to the broad fields of educational and cognitive research, let us not forget that the research itself did not offer up the strategies and routines that work in our classroom. Our teachers did that. The research around instructional best practices simply affirms and then synthesizes for us the techniques that our best teachers use. Great teaching comes first, and the research follows. Come to think of it, each one of our best practices began with an innovative teacher in some classroom somewhere who decided to try something new, who was determined to reach just one more child, and to save one more life. Let us not forget that every best practice began as a new practice.

At some point in our lives, each of us has been inspired by and forever changed by the expertise and artistry of our teachers. It is not an overstatement to say that we owe all substantive advancements in education and the lives of many children to the passionate teachers who have mastered their craft, with each step observed and affirmed by thousands of classroom visits and countless research studies. This brings us to a frustrating and confusing paradox. While the success of children remains in the deft hands of caring teachers, the very ones who matter most in this equation are being questioned and criticized more than ever.

This is a hard reality that we cannot unsee, though not one that we cannot undo. The era of federal and state accountability and high-stakes testing has been a reckless attempt to standardize and marginalize children and teachers. It has brought forth misinformed and unsuccessful attempts to replicate great instruction, from asynchronous learning models to online reading and math programs. While these tools have value, they cannot provide what comes only from teachers. We have learned through study and practice that technology can supplement the work of skilled teachers, but it cannot replace it. We must admit that and do better.

In celebration of teachers everywhere, this book attempts to pinpoint what works in classrooms without the tricks and shortcuts. It draws on teacher guidance and best practice to distinguish the nice-to-know strategies from the high-impact ones. More than that, it dares to isolate the no-doubt-about-it, talk-to-the-hand most effective techniques (described via this text as "force-multipliers") that accelerate learning for all children no matter their backgrounds.

There is no doubt that if we filled a room full of master teachers via some kind of escape room exercise, they would solve the challenges we face in education. That is something that neither the policymakers nor the researchers can do. In that spirit, it is time again to renew our purpose as educators and regain our souls. With the great tapestry of education still unfolding before us, let us contribute to what it may someday become. Along that journey, let us reestablish our trust and belief in teachers, reject the current attacks on our schools, reinstall the strategies that work best for our children, reinspire our faith, and re-wonder again.

Acknowledgments

The idea of a guidebook for building confidence and creativity within students is formed from an endless array of conversations I have had with top-notch teachers and innovative leaders who are boldly searching for the right answers in service to children and families. There are too many people to name here, but each one of my long-standing colleagues has contributed to this book in some way. I hope that the ideas provided in this text draw upon our shared victories and collective missteps, and that they honor the sacrifice of our good deeds.

I am infinitely grateful to the kind folks at Bloomsbury Publishing who believed in this project from the start. My first book *The Instructional Soul: Leading Schools with a Spirit of Innovation* (2019) was crafted as a what-we-might-someday-become commentary on education, with a fair amount of systems theory and cognitive science tossed in. This book puts those ideas into practice. It is provided as a how-to guide for shaping schools with teacher leadership and student voice as centerpieces. This book is inspired by the notion that dramatic system change is possible, and it offers practical steps for teachers and principals who are in the work now and itching to get moving.

As always, I thank my family for listening to all the ideas I toss around for improving education, and for their well-played humor about my desire to read dusty old books and retell unfunny dad jokes. I thank my colleagues as well for pushing me to write another book. They made me promise to offer up practical advice and suggestions because those who work hard in our schools each day deserve a book that honors their craft and helps them accomplish great things on behalf of kids. I pray that this book makes good on that promise and that it serves you well.

Introduction

We remain a world of dreamers and doers. These are uniquely human qualities that give us purpose and separate us from other living creatures. Children embody these curious ponderings from their earliest days, watching intently as some silly adult waves a rattle back and forth. In these brief moments of discovery and wondering, children absorb all the noise and commotion around them, eyes open wide with great intent to understand what is happening and the possibilities that they bring. Yes, we are all deeply curious beings, and we all dream. As educators in our schools, we owe children an instructional experience that is faithful to those dreams.

This book is written in service to such things. It is designed as a guidebook for teachers who need a place to start, for those of us who want more for our students than they are experiencing now. This text attempts to recenter our work around students, first and foremost. It begins by addressing their wants and needs, along with a core belief that teachers are the ones who can get us there. To be clear, the beliefs that underscore everything presented in this book are as follows:

1. That teachers are central to all good things in education and that they must be positioned to lead our industry moving forward.
2. That all children can learn and succeed at very high levels no matter their backgrounds and home environments.

In honor of those who know best, this book amplifies the expertise of teachers as the key agents for how we build schools that are future-ready and student-centered. As a critical step in that direction, the upcoming chapters propose a move away from the current accountability structures and measures that have defined our students and teachers as a series of scale scores and percentile rankings. Sorting children is ineffective and silly, and we have known that all along. If we design a new way forward, we can pinpoint the right mix of classroom strategies and experiences that lead to self-actualized learners who imbue academic confidence, personal clarity, and creative purpose. In unequivocable and practical terms, the following chapters provide the key teacher moves, instructional methods, and classroom conditions that must be in place for deep and meaningful learning to happen no matter a student's ambitions or struggles.

Chapter 1 challenges our current systems born out of legislative mandates that can make learning rote and transactional (assignments, grades, and rank-ordering) and invites a more meaningful and inspirational experience for children (explicit, applied, and learner-centered) that is within our reach if we really want it. Chapter 2 summarizes and simplifies the no-doubt-about-it, best-of-the-best instructional practices that teachers must employ to ensure learning for all students because schooling must function first-and-foremost to accelerate academic achievement. Chapter 3 explains the key actions necessary to connect curriculum to community in ways that enhance student lives inside and outside of school because students are rightly demanding a learning experience that is highly relevant and deeply personal. Chapter 4 explores the relationship between core content acquisition, creative expression, and workplace skills that students need to succeed beyond the classroom because learning must accentuate each student's strengths and embolden their place and purpose in the world. Chapter 5 emphasizes the need for innovative leadership and bold decision-making if we are to build great schools that are models for honest-to-God engagement because the changes we seek are within our reach if we have the courage to see around the bend, if we believe in the things that we say, and if we dare them to be.

1 The Promise of Children

Because I criticize a system, they think I criticize them—and that is of course because they accept the system and identify themselves with it.

—Thomas Merton, Poet

Nothing is more certain among educators than a common, unerring belief in the promise of children. In fact, their promise is our practice. Just as no one can doubt the capacity of a child to grow up and do amazing things, we can never underestimate the impact of our teachers as the central agents in getting them there. If that is true, then our belief and investment in teachers has never been more critical. Every attempt to outsmart and outsource teachers has failed. As an industry, our collective mission cannot be any clearer. Hire and train great teachers, celebrate and honor their work, and don't ever doubt them.

Public education is ever evolving, and that is an exciting place for us to be. The future of schooling will involve more flexible scheduling options, more applied curricula, and more authentic student voice. Still, none of these things will be successful in the absence of great teachers and their command of explicit instructional practices.

The perils of public education continue to dominate social media debates and have given rise to new questions about our future and fresh threats to our profession. This has taken a toll on teachers, undermining their worth and value. In fact, if we lean in a bit closer, we will hear an impassioned cry from many teachers who are on the verge of emotional collapse. Their requests for fewer initiatives, more time, and fair wages have gone unaddressed for far too long and let that be a lesson to those in leadership. Our teachers, staff, and students are telling us what they want and need. In response, it is time that we speak less and listen more, an especially important lesson for those in our state legislatures and school district offices.

If we dare to listen, we will hear a common refrain from teachers about standards and benchmarks that feel disconnected or irrelevant. We will hear some not-so-subtle critiques of top-down accountability and standardized testing as reckless experiments that benefit politicians and policymakers more than students and families. We will hear stories about a lack of trust and community in our schools, about increased isolation among our students, and about the compounding emotional struggles that threaten our students and staff.

Not So Fast, My Friend

The good news is that the solutions we seek are within our control. Still, getting us to a place of affirmation, promise, and hope will not come without resistance. The turnstile of new initiatives and accountability mandates will not lessen anytime soon. That is why it feels as if our teachers and principals are running down the escalator in hopes of catching the subway train, only to find it left the station long ago. They find themselves lost and unsure of where to turn. In a desperate attempt to do something, they frantically chase the train down the tunnel, tossing in its way more parts, more solutions, and more people and policies in an endless spray of graffiti that to some may look like artwork but to the rest of us is nothing more than institutional vandalism.

A more empowering solution will require us to reclaim our voices as educators and restore our trust in school models that are exhilarating and transformative. It will demand that teachers and administrators reshape our work in tribute to what schools could someday become, thrilling centers for collaboration, experimentation, and enrichment for both students and teachers. To be clear, accountability in some form is necessary. Still, the rigid state-sponsored models we see across the nation have left little room for creative expression and instructional innovation. These structures are just plain suffocating for everyone involved. While we can find pockets of success here and there, bringing innovation to scale has been hindered by layers and layers of legislative mandates and bureaucratic silliness.

It is high time that we spoke with a unified voice in declaring that the era of federal and state accountability is over, that the stifling systems of oversight in place across the land have failed miserably, and that our teachers and students have been heard in their plea for something that means so much more. The question about whether high-stakes accountability has worked to improve our schools has been asked and answered. The lofty promises of state-sponsored assessment and school ranking metrics have been oversold, and the results are underwhelming. Though achievement has increased marginally, there has been little benefit to reducing racial achievement gaps and no scalable solutions for schools have resulted (Ordofa and Asgedom 2022, 100358; Hanushek and Raymond 2005, 297–327).

It is not surprising to learn that scores can increase in response to top-down mandates, intimidation tactics, and fear of losing one's job. Still, the tradeoffs are predictable and painful. For every successful turnaround school, there are many that have either crumbled from the weight or sold out in search of academic gain. Along the way, we have scared away good and caring teachers, and deprived children of their dignity.

Come to think of it, the idea of applying a rigid business model to public schooling was a bad idea from the start, with all due respect to those who tried valiantly to make it work. As author and essayist, Robert Fulghum warned us, "An idea not worth doing is worth not doing well" (Fulghum 2004). No one can doubt the need for accountability in our schools, but we should not confuse our belief in individual responsibility with state-sponsored bureaucracy. Top-down management structures have never been correlated with quality schooling anyway. They came about after a long history of pressures from non-educators to reform the system by putting more people in charge and creating more boxes to check (Good 1962; Kliebard 2004).

The history of K-12 schools in America was formed from a loose collection of one-room schoolhouses. Those were messy days, indeed. Little structure led to great variance and even chaos in some schools. Teachers were not credentialed, and some students did not learn very much. This led to a gross overcorrection to standardize teacher training, curriculum materials, and achievement outcomes, all of which were pushed by politicians and university professors. Nearly everyone called for someone to oversee school quality, inspect the work, and tightly measure results. The solution was the school superintendent (Good 1962).

Somewhere in the move to centralized school systems, our politicians, policymakers, and even superintendents became more trusting of top-down solutions. Along the way, the entire educational system became less personal and more critical. We lost sight of the uniqueness of the individual child. We valued our teachers less. We did not involve our families. We trusted data outcomes, even when the results were illogical or redundant or ran counter to what we observed with our own eyes. We leaned less and less on our expertise as educators and even questioned our beliefs about what effective schooling looked like. We lost touch with our creative spirit, and lost sight of our instructional souls.

We have been doing it this way for so long and are in so deep that any alternative idea can sound naïve or irrational. This is where leadership comes in, both from teachers and administrators. With their guidance, we can restore our commitment to a set of educational values as a starting point for change. Some of those value statements might include the following: *All students will achieve at high levels. Teacher expertise and voice will be valued. Classroom strategies will be explicit and effective. Time and space for deep collaboration will be prioritized. Civic involvement will be fostered. Student self-efficacy will be affirmed. And just maybe, reading and writing will be fun again.* While this work will be daunting, it will also be rewarding. It will be empowering for teachers and fulfilling for kids.

How to Get There: Pulling the Right Levers

To advance our work, educators must reestablish their influence, and that means agreeing on what matters most. The research on instructional best practices and school improvement provides a good place to start. Just as important, we have reliable observational data from thousands upon thousands of classroom visits across the globe that have given us specific strategies that we know work because we have seen them in action. All of this leads us to an unmistakable conclusion: We know what works in schools, and we know what doesn't.

This book attempts to summarize those things that work best in a way that gives us confidence that we can lead the work moving forward, without the need for top-down management and without turning core instruction over to computers. The question about what works in schools has been answered many times, as long as we listen to researchers and practitioners alike. In the end, we must acknowledge and leverage both the art and science of teaching. Our best teachers are artisans, with a deep understanding of their materials and techniques, and with a keen eye to execute and refine their actions at precisely the right moments. Across our industry, we have leaned heavily on published research summaries and given less attention to the empirical evidence we have from watching and listening to teachers. In fact, it is perplexing that many of us trust the conclusions of a researcher who has never taught anyone more than we do the successful teacher down the hallway. We have been conditioned to trust the scientists who study teaching and learning even when the experts are in our own buildings.

It is time then for a get-off-our-backs approach to teaching and a get-off-my-lawn approach to leadership. Localized school control that puts decisions about curriculum, assessment, scheduling, and grading in the hands of teachers and principals will breed innovative models and reconnect schools to their communities. Leading in this way comes with the responsibility of knowing and executing best practices that must undergird our plans. If we want to own the changes in our schools, we must be informed about what works so we are confident and credible in our actions. As a way forward, the following high-leverage techniques and classroom routines are presented in the upcoming chapters as the most influential and impactful in building creative and confident students:

- Teacher Modeling
- Academic Discussion
- Writing and Note-Taking
- Practice and Error Analysis
- Spiraled Review and Re-Teaching
- Cultural Awareness
- Emotional Wellness
- Content Relevance
- Applied Learning
- Student Voice.

These ten actions (which we will call "levers") are both functional and logical, and each one is commonly observed among our best teachers as integral to any successful classroom.

The list is provided as a way of simplifying and clarifying the immediate action items that must be in place and central to our work if we want all students to be academically successful and emotionally confident. Of course, any attempt to make a list is done knowing the quizzical looks and questions that always come with it. To be clear, the order of the items is unimportant, and some of them have more influence on achievement than others. For example, designing relevant lessons is critical to building meaningful learning experiences but is not as important to mastering course content as having students involved in robust academic discussion. For this reason, it is best to view the first five as learning levers, and the next five as engagement levers. To put it another way, the first five are surefire techniques to increase academic achievement and student self-confidence, while the next five are critical actions to improve student self-esteem and self-expression.

The levers are provided as action items for teachers and leaders who are looking for the right moves to impact learning quickly and powerfully. They are summarized and explained to help teachers who are in search of methods they can trust to be effective in supporting all learners. They are derived from an exhaustive review of evidence-based practices that are familiar to most educators (e.g., Marzano), and they are consistently observed in effective classrooms across all grade levels.

Still, the list is not presented as preferable to any other collection of best practices. This list is provided only to narrow our focus on the following: (i) Those actions that are commonly shown to impact academic achievement (explicit and effective) and (ii) The techniques that promote student well-being, creativity, and voice (applied and meaningful). This list draws on the inventories of evidence-based strategies that educators know well (e.g., Marzano). As such, it honors the conclusions of the most renowned researchers in our industry. The list leans heavily on the most prominent analyses and meta-analyses on teacher practice and school reform that we have available (e.g., Hattie). Each of the levers is tightly aligned to high-yield effect sizes and cross-referenced with observed practices that are commonly used among highly effective teachers. The levers attempt to capture best practices in a way that makes sense to practitioners in our schools. It condenses a laundry list of strategies that teachers use down to a handful that are most impactful, and it highlights some practices that are needed to build the kind of student-centered schools that we envision.

Each one of the levers is a critical attribute to a successful classroom. As such, the practices listed were not randomly selected, and they are not just conversation-starters. These are must-do actions. The essential pedagogy. The absolutes. Though some can be combined or renamed, none can be eliminated. The descriptions and order of the levers can shift to your liking, but each one is a unique classroom practice that needs the others to create the lessons and activities that our students require. Let's put it this way: We simply cannot have great schools if students leave us having mastered their reading and math skills, but they cannot tie a knot or pitch a new idea. We cannot consider it successful to graduate a student at the top of their class if they leave us emotionally unwell or culturally devoid.

It would be inaccurate to describe these practices as a list of strategies, though there are many strategies that fit nicely under each one. It is better to describe them as high impact methods or levers that (when pulled at the right times) lead to deep learning and high achievement no matter the unique strengths of individual students. Each of the levers is presented and explained with current practitioners in mind, for those who are sitting in a media center somewhere working on a school improvement plan or for those who are meeting as a professional learning community (PLC) in a cramped teacher workroom drinking lukewarm coffee and staring at data tables. As such, the levers are presented in a manner that is manageable for teachers who have a lot on their plates.

Each lever is described in the upcoming chapters, with classroom examples given and cautions provided. The descriptions are meant to inform and empower teachers and administrators who are trying hard to get it right, who are listening to a lot of advice and reading a lot of books, and who are sorting out what matters most. In the spirit of innovative school models and engaging lesson design, these levers push our work forward in meeting the demands of students for more relevant topics and lessons and more creative ways to showcase their learning. It is hopeful that these practices ground our discussion around what is best for students and promote healthy debate among professionals as we endeavor to build the type of schools we all want and identify the instructional pre-qualifiers needed for students to inch closer to what Maslow described as self-actualization.

Maslow Whisperers / What the Hierarchy Is Really Telling Us

Maslow's hierarchy is to educators what girth is to sumo wrestlers—far-reaching and essential. For years, we have planned our teacher professional development in part around his famous pyramid model (see Figure 1.1). Surprisingly, the focus has been almost exclusively on the bottom rungs. That is where Maslow famously claims that no real learning or human advancement can come without feeling first safe and loved. As any educator will tell you, there is nothing more foundational than that. In keeping with

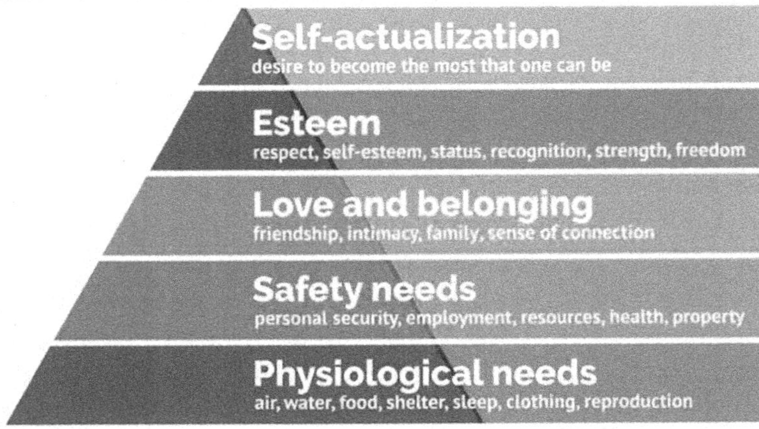

Figure 1.1 *Maslow's hierarchy of needs.*

Maslow's hierarchy, we know that we must attend to each student's human needs as well as their academic ones.

Still, here's the rub. The most important gift we can provide to children is the assurance that their foundational skills are sound, that they are learning grade-level content, and that their higher-order reasoning skills are top notch. Why? Because no amount of caring for our students is a substitute for helping them gain academic skills and confidence. And here's the good news: We can actually teach in a way that ensures academic achievement and promotes confidence, and those instructional practices do not limit our abilities to value students and keep them safe.

To be honest, we have to wonder whether the base rungs of Maslow's hierarchy are where our deficit thinking creeps in. It is fair to ponder whether we spend so much time tending to the emotional needs of our students that we sometimes view learning as secondary to caring, as if they represent two disparate outcomes. Even worse, it may be true that we value academic achievement for all students, but we view it as unattainable for some because so many arrive to class with so much baggage. For whatever reason, scant attention has been paid across our industry to the top layers of Maslow's model, with all due respect to those of us who believe we are helping kids by loving them to death. There is no doubt that we need to make all students feel safe and welcome, but the end game is confidence. This chicken-and-egg dilemma in education is real and not easily solved. Educators love to debate which one comes first, student relationships or academic rigor. It might be more helpful to consider whether one can exist without the other.

This is a reminder that formal schooling runs parallel to student home environments, and simultaneously with things like puberty and teenage angst. Though our work in schools is critically important, we are not the only source for learning. Students learn a great deal at home and in their neighborhoods. In fact, it can be argued that life is the core content, and schooling is just a supplemental curriculum. This may explain in part why so many children dislike school. Some may view their lessons as not only irrelevant to their lives, but as counter to their needs. This is why forcing rigorous assignments on students (high expectations) does not ensure learning in the absence of real-life examples and cultural connections (content relevance). It is fair to ask whether students view things like self-worth and pride as more vital than content knowledge in meeting their current needs (see Maslow's higher rungs). These social-emotional competencies are developed not by reading and studying but by doing (applied learning) and saying (student voice).

Research and experience do not typically lead us astray. As an example, professional wisdom and logic tell us that academic acceleration (challenging students) is more effective than remediation (underchallenging them), for no child should be exempt from exceptionalism. If so, then the promise of academic excellence for all places responsibilities on us to do more (not less) for those students who we worry about the most. In fact, it could mean that some students are underperforming not because of something they have done (or not done), but in response to what we have done in designing their curriculum and lessons. In his book *Why Don't Students Like School?*, cognitive scientist Daniel Willingham puts it this way: "People are naturally curious, but we are not naturally good thinkers; unless the cognitive conditions are right, we will avoid thinking" (Willingham 2010, 3).

The litmus test is knowing that we have the right conditions in place for students to gain confidence each year they are in school. For the true

Table 1.1 High-Impact Classroom Levers

Academic Confidence	Personal Clarity	Creative Purpose
Teacher Modeling	Cultural Awareness	Applied Learning
Academic Discussion	Emotional Wellness	Student Voice
Writing and Note-Taking	Content Relevance	
Practice and Error-Analysis		
Spiraled Review and Re-Teaching		

validation of our success as educators is the degree that we advance students through a system that provides increasing confidence, purpose, and hope. This is absolutely within our control, and the levers provided represent the no-doubt-about-it methods to get students there (see Table 1.1).

Tradition and Truth Ain't the Same Things

Whatever steps we take, we will be more successful if we narrow our focus to a few key things and get those right first and foremost. That means resisting the temptation to take on more tasks than we can do effectively. We must also be truthful about what really works in schools. That will require us to revisit what we spend our time on that is simply not working. This is a hard topic for us to discuss as educators because we all have our favorite strategies and routines. The truth is that they don't all work so well, and we must be open to trying some others.

As hard as it is to hear, we may have to admit that we have some bad habits. Yes, this is beginning to feel like a new diet. Still, the analogy is a good one because we know that eating salad is better for us than eating fried chicken. This is a matter of truth, not opinion. The challenge for us is to accept the things we know to be true and form good habits or just give up on what is best and eat the dang chicken. Either way, we are making choices and there are consequences.

Each of us forms habits as a way of feeling more secure and in control, whether that means writing a daily "To Do" list or planning our meals days in advance. In forming our routines, we convince ourselves that they work best for us and (here we go) that we are not ready to risk a shift to something else. Any change to our habits usually comes after some kicking and screaming. To be honest, many of us would never have jumped into online ordering, virtual banking, artificial intelligence, and dozens of other advancements if someone didn't force our hands. A teenager simply cannot understand why his parents will not download the latest app that makes traveling easier to manage, and why his grandparents are content to place their orders at the counter when ordering ahead on their phones makes it so much faster. Examples like these are many, even when they are illogical.

The same is true in our schools. We do many routine tasks out of habits that are formed from experience as we evolve from a wobbly, uncertain new teacher to a proud, accomplished veteran. It is not an exaggeration to say that much of what we do as teachers begins in our early years as survival techniques, from the way we ask questions to the way we hand out papers. This is the benefit of experience, and most of the time it doesn't fail us. All professional habits in all industries are inspired by our wants and needs, informed through study and practice, and codified by time.

If someone comes along to offer a new idea, we tend to listen politely and then remind them that our habits work for us but thanks anyway. If that isn't enough, we are quick to quote a random research study to back our claims. In education, it is hard to know what to focus on because there are so many strategies in play across schools and classrooms, and so many opinions being shared. The long-standing and ongoing debate about the best way to teach reading is just one of many examples. This is why it is critically important for educators to build their practices on the advice of research that they themselves have reviewed, and on the backs of practices that they themselves have seen in action.

On one hand, the education industry has a long history of adopting new ideas, shortcutting their implementation, labeling them as ineffective, and abandoning them quickly. On the other hand, our industry passes down from one generation to the next a list of practices that we all assume are effective and that no one takes the time to question anymore. As a result, we sometimes spend a lot of time training and perfecting techniques that are certainly not harmful to students but are not advancing their learning and engagement. Some examples include time-honored traditions like classroom seating arrangements, student scheduling options, grade point averages, class rankings, and even mentoring.

There is nothing inherently wrong with any of these structures, but the time and effort we spend on them may not provide as much return on student achievement as we think. In many schools, the strategic actions we put into place to impact learning are either long-standing traditions that no one has thought to change or deep-seated professional preferences that someone in charge has convinced us are too important to mess with. This is not a criticism; it is simply a caution. Here's the thing to know: Conventional wisdom and truth are not the same things. Just because we have been doing it this way for a long time (conventional), and just because our colleagues are saying the same things (wisdom), doesn't mean the things we are doing are best practices (truth).

What Our Gut Might Be Telling Us

As leaders and experts in this work, we have got to trust our gut sometimes. We are so programmed to lean on research that we sometimes put into practice routines that don't mesh with what our instincts are telling us. Those gut feelings come from a place of expertise and experience that we cannot deny. Let's consider a favorite topic to debate: standardized testing. Isn't it true that just about everyone who works in schools has a sense that standardized testing is not good for kids? Though we can list some arguments in favor of it—it levels the playing field (which it can), it provides good data (which it can)—there is something about standardized testing that doesn't feel right to educators. While it may have a place in our schools, it has been oversold and overutilized. There are many practices like this that have shifted over time, a few others that have come and gone, and even some that are illogical and counter intuitive. Let's look at two examples.

Classroom Examples:

- **Independent Reading.** Any teacher will tell you that students who read more become better readers. Still, the research around independent reading in school is mixed and professional opinions vary greatly. If you are unsure, try asking someone about reading stations, reading logs, round-robin reading, drop everything and read programs, and even reading at home and see the reactions you get. Most are convinced that extant research doesn't support these practices. Some of us are so passionate about these beliefs that we give very little time over to independent reading during the school day. As a result, we see fewer classrooms where students are reading books that interest them, and we rarely see students called on to read aloud. Many teachers have moved away from independent reading over concerns that some students are faking it or maybe that the time is better spent annotating more rigorous texts. These are worthy discussions, but it is fair to wonder if there is more to consider on this topic. Our gut tells us that students should be reading more, but our actions have them reading less.
- **Student Homework.** A similar trend has emerged around homework, which many schools have dropped completely because it is viewed as inequitable for those students who come from less affluent families. While no one can argue this point, it is hard to say that students would not benefit by reading more at home or reviewing their times tables.

> Any teacher will tell you that students need more time to practice, not less. It is fair to question whether the type of homework we provide is valuable or just busy work, but that doesn't alter the need for students to practice skills when they are not in school. It could be true that our passions around this topic might be stalling our solutions in trying to make homework assignments more valuable and equitable instead of tossing it out and declaring it no longer a best practice.

These examples are not meant to slight the research nor to ridicule the professional opinions that guide our work. They are highlighted to show how conventional thinking shifts over time and drives our actions in schools, even when those opinions are not fully backed by science or supported by our best practitioners. While some of the concerns around reading, homework, and many other practices are valid, teachers and administrators must continue to study these things for themselves and then trust their instincts.

Professional debate should not make us less reliant on educational research. The research should inform our debate, but it should not settle it for us. It is important that we understand the limitations of the results of a single experiment and even among several valid studies. The research on learning (i.e., the science of learning) is a fascinating topic and provides the foundation for much of what is discussed in this book. Still, the educational and cognitive sciences are still evolving so it is prudent not to generalize the findings. Let's remember that some of the practices we do in schools have only a few studies to draw from, and others have not been studied at all. Even the most prominent meta-analyses we have on instructional practices produce effect sizes that only approximate the impact on students. It is best to think of these findings as the average impact on the average student. In fact, some of the research even goes so far as to average the averages. This is why we should review the research but not follow it blindly. Classroom trial and error should also guide what we do, as well as learning from those who are getting great results. It only makes sense that we learn from the teachers and principals who are doing exceedingly well, and to reflect on and replicate their practices.

When the Solutions Are the Problem

The greatest challenges we face in education are rooted in our proudest solutions. This irony is played out every day across our schools, and it is part of the reason that change in our industry comes slowly and with bitter disagreement. The most prominent example of this is a belief among educators that school is the most powerful social agent in helping each child reach their unique potential, in leveling the playing field, and increasing opportunity for all. In response, we have built a system that is designed to standardize how children learn, what teachers teach, how they teach it, and how it is measured. The system sorts and rank-orders all things and then labels anything near the bottom as unsuccessful and unworthy. Those at the bottom simply did not, or cannot, survive the system, and the system blames them for this.

This is what results from a system where standardized testing is put in place not as a tool, but as the outcome itself. In the end, we spend a lot of time teaching students to locate the answers that we have determined are the right ones. Alas, school is not really about the students and meeting their needs. In providing an historical perspective, educational philosopher and reformer John Dewey implored educators and policymakers more than a hundred years ago to keep their focus on teaching students how to think. As Dewey described it, schools are designed to help students learn to learn (Dewey [1916] 2018).

The latest research on how we "learn to learn" comes from psychology and cognitive science under titles like self-efficacy. What is fascinating about this research is that self-efficacy is described as more than a belief in oneself. True self-efficacy requires that our confidence in ourselves be tied to a belief that we can control our futures, our own destinies (Orth and Robins 2022, 5–17). This is more than simple optimism. It is orchestrated confidence. It is operational self-actualization, because we have designed the systems required to get our students there.

Though we are often well-intentioned, we have made the mistake many times of implementing something without considering the side effects. Our efforts to standardize what students should learn have led us to a place where we standardize everything from what is posted in our classrooms to how our students take notes. Think about how that runs counter to what we preach about individualism and creative purpose. Our industry is replete with ironies like these that are so entrenched that we don't even notice them. As we move forward, two such examples require our attention:

- An industry designed around people (teachers and students) and purely human outputs (skills, intelligence, kindness) has created accountability systems and metrics that seem more suited to building cars than kids.

- An industry designed to facilitate intellectualism and creativity has created curricula, assessments, and structures that limit experimentation, social interaction, and voice.

In her brilliant introduction to Dewey's classic text *Democracy and Education*, professor and author Patricia H. Hinchey presents educators with this challenge: "The kind of citizens that schools educate will shape the kind of society the country becomes tomorrow" (Dewey [1916] 2018). She cautions that expecting students to read, deliberate, and answer in the same way has created a generation of students who lack the skill and confidence to solve things for themselves.

> The need for high test scores has emphasized a very specific style of reading: reading for the sake of answering test questions. This is a perversion of what many experts consider "reading." Whereas literacy experts say the point of reading is to make sense of a text for oneself, students in testing environments learn instead that the point of reading is to extract—often to guess—answers to questions by far distant faceless and nameless test makers, even answers to questions and reading passages that themselves make no sense at all. The result is that college classrooms currently teem with students who have little or no practice in reading as an effort to make personal sense of a text, and they are flummoxed when they are simply told "Read this." (Dewey [1916] 2018, xviii)

Let's peek inside a classroom and see how this might play out (see Table 1.2).

What does all this mean? It means that while formal schooling is established to impart skills and knowledge, students need just as much socialization as they do education. In fact, the former is more important to most of us in our daily lives. It is fair to say that human beings do not seek to be smart as much as they seek to be accepted. In response, the curriculum and lessons we design should help students become who they want to be, not who we want them to be. So, yet another irony emerges. While adults are hyper-focused on designing a system where children grow up to be successful, children seek only a world where they have purpose.

Scholar and theologian C. S. Lewis cautioned us about the dangers of teaching children to locate only the right answers, themes, or symbols as the teacher has predetermined. He notes that students who do not give "the right responses to the right authors" in school are oftentimes corrected. Over time, some children become conditioned to search not for their own insights but only for the answers that meet with the teacher's approval. As such, a

Table 1.2 Teacher Dilemma: Reading Routines

Inside the Classroom: A Closer Look
• In a fifth grade classroom, Mrs. Crandle has heard from her administrator and grade-level team that students need to spend more time analyzing rigorous texts so they can be ready for the state assessment. Mrs. Crandle has located a set of challenging passages from the district curriculum, along with training on close reading strategies that students must master. While students routinely practice as they are told, Mrs. Crandle notices that many of her students are bored and some are frustrated with these routines. They want to read for pleasure and take notes in a way that works for them. Mrs. Crandle asks them to stick to the methods she has taught them, and she presses on. She notices that her students are getting better at repeating back the themes of the text that she believes are correct. Her students master the reading routines, and they have become quite skilled at giving Mrs. Crandle the answers she wants. The problem is, they don't like reading as much as they used to.
Considerations and Solutions
• Mrs. Crandle has not received bad advice. It is true that her students need to be pushed by reading challenging texts. Students will almost always rise to the level of the tasks placed before them, and making school easy for children is not helping them.
• **To increase engagement in her classroom**, Mrs. Crandle might track down and utilize challenging passages that are interesting to her students. She might even give them a choice of which rigorous text they want to tackle, first by themselves and then in small groups based on the text they choose. The teacher might provide a passage about space exploration, another about deep water submarines, another about women's suffrage, and yet another about a community's fight to save an historic theatre. The key here is that the entire class does not need to read the same passage. In the end, the goal has to be equal parts skill-building and interest-building so students see reading as fascinating and not frustrating.
• **To increase her students' skills and confidence**, Mrs. Crandle might ask each student to unpack the theme of the text or to summarize the text in their own words and with their own evidence. Her focus at the onset is not to ensure the right responses but to develop the right habits for close reading. She could utilize a check for understanding strategy that asks some students to read aloud and justify their responses, and then she can provide real-time feedback for them to improve their answers. Mrs. Crandle could also provide her own insights, conclusions, and evidence for each of the passages, but only after the students have provided theirs. This gives the teacher an opportunity to model her own thinking and attack strategies that work best for her, and that students could utilize for themselves.

student views their ideas as less valued and sees things like reading poetry or solving math problems as just onerous tasks that we are made to do in school. Lewis puts it this way: "Those who read poetry to improve their minds will never improve their minds by reading poetry. For the true enjoyments must be spontaneous and compulsive and look to no remoter end. The Muses will submit to no marriage of convenience" (Lewis 1952, 35).

Conventional ways of doing schooling can shift if we are bold enough to own the solutions moving forward. This will require us to trust our teachers and principals and encourage them to innovate with time, place, and purpose within reasonable boundaries. It will require us as well to listen to our instincts and trust our experience because we know that students do not like nor do they benefit from things like test prep activities even if they raise achievement scores. It means we must do more authentic reading and writing, more applied science and math, more initiatives in our local communities, and more learning outside.

If we can create such experiences, students will arrive each day less focused on grades and assessments and more immersed in a marketplace of learning, where debate is encouraged, civility is fostered, and resourcefulness is nourished. In education, that work cannot begin without a dedicated review of what we have learned from giants like Dewey and Maslow who sought to push our school experiences beyond basic skills and toward the grander desires of knowing who we are and how we learn. This is an entry point for restoring the soul of the system.

School Is About Them, Not Us

If Maslow were here, he would tell us that every human being can aspire to self-actualization (though it is rare to accomplish). He went so far as to study and name those who he believed reached the pinnacle of self-actualization during their lifetimes, including Albert Einstein and Abraham Lincoln. While most of us will never reach those levels of notoriety, our schools would be wise to consider how to establish systems that push students to loftier heights of academic confidence (see Chapter 2), personal clarity (see Chapter 3), and creative purpose (see Chapter 4). Anything less feels sadly unambitious.

Let us be clear. If we design schools to improve state-imposed metrics, we will focus on some students more than others, we will value some teachers more than others, and we will celebrate some schools more than others. On the contrary, if we design schools that are teacher-led and student-focused, we are pushed to conceive of classrooms and lessons where teachers like teaching, where students thrive at all costs, where learning (not teaching) is our nucleus, and where any child who underperforms is seen as unacceptable (even unfathomable). In doing so, we will wrest back control of our schools, burst the shackles of accountability, and breathe in the fresh air of academic freedom.

2 Building Academic Confidence

If you can show me how I can cling to that which is real to me, while teaching me a way into the larger society, then I will not only drop my defenses and my hostility, but I will sing your praises, and I will help to make the desert bear fruit.

—Ralph Ellison, Author and Activist

Confidence is not given. It is earned. Whether we are talking about an adult who is learning a new hobby (e.g., painting, golf, pickleball) or a student learning a new skill (e.g., reading, spelling, fractions), confidence is gained through repeated practice and success. There is no shortcut. In fact, if we peeled the purpose of schooling to its core, we would find that we are not in the content business. We are in the confidence business. Nothing is more exhilarating than watching young people grow in confidence. Our career satisfaction is fulfilled when we see a highly skilled, confident young person moving from elementary school to middle school and then graduating from high school with years and years of knowledge and purpose that we helped to cultivate. As we watch this scene unfold in our schools, we see the culmination of our work as educators. It gives us hope that the future is in good hands, and that we had a say in it.

With that in mind, it is both a responsibility and privilege to create lessons that build academic confidence and mold unrefined young children into self-actualized adults. To get us started, let us try to picture a young child entering kindergarten at five years old, attending formal schooling for the first time with emerging language skills and a great deal of curiosity about the world around them. There is so much they do not yet know, and there are countless school and home experiences that will arrive over many years. What those young children will learn and how they view themselves over the course of their lives is something we will shape. Make no mistake about the importance of our work as educators. What they become will not arrive by accident, but by design.

It is not a stretch to say that our school experiences determine our fates, with all due respect to the importance of parenting. In fact, let us picture again that eager kindergarten student many years later, after hundreds and hundreds of lessons that we designed. Will that student graduate from high school more confident and curious than the day they arrived in kindergarten? One would think so, but this is not always the case. As painful as it is to hear, we see students move through our schools and become less confident along the way. We see students enter our school systems as wide-eyed and eager young learners, only to find those same students many years later with poor grades and lousy self-esteem.

Those students who were once excited to be in school no longer read as much, speak as much, or laugh as much. They are a little less curious. They are less silly. It is a hard truth to know that many children journey through a system that leaves them more skeptical, more frustrated, less trusting, and less hopeful. We simply cannot let that happen. Yes, it is true that the true validation of our worth as educators is the degree by which we advance children through a system that provides them with confidence, purpose, and hope. The good news is this: We can design such a system.

If the classroom experiences in school were fully in our control (which they are), we would design a series of learning activities that heighten student curiosity and slowly build their confidence. If we were truly student-focused, we would provide each child with whatever they needed to be highly skilled and self-aware, and we would design tasks that promote those attributes over time. The extant research on human growth and development backs up this claim. A review of the science shows that people with high self-esteem typically have more success at school and work, better social relationships, improved mental and physical health, and less antisocial behavior. And these benefits persist from adolescence to adulthood and into old age (Orth and Robins 2022, 5–17).

As educators, it is important to know that simply telling someone to be happier or to feel better about themselves does not work. This is especially true of children. Students are inherently skeptical of what they hear from adults so they must experience success in order to trust it. When a Little League coach tells a player to be more confident when they are not or that they are good at something when they are not, their words are well-intentioned but not helpful. In fact, when we exaggerate how proud we are of students, they often don't believe it. While authentic praise is critical to human growth, false praise is detrimental. When we offer false praise, students can sense it. We are not fooling them. They are on to us.

Seeding Confidence in Our Classrooms

We have clear research and indisputable evidence that shows the impact of great teachers in growing academic success (Sanders and Rivers 1996). While this may be difficult for newer teachers to hear, it is true that our veteran teachers know a few tricks that the rest of us do not. The good news is that the process for learning something new is not really that complicated. We have thousands of years of experience that show us how, along with countless studies that have affirmed these practices over and over again. For example, we know that poverty negatively impacts learning and that practicing something positively impacts it. We know that asking great questions leads to deeper learning, while posing easy questions does not. We also know that there is a big difference between a teacher who covers the course content and one who ensures that all students have learned it.

What may be most encouraging and distressing at the same time is this reality: We design the systems by which our students learn, and so only we can remake them. We create the lessons so the idea of building classroom activities that ensure student mastery of content and skill is within our control. Though any person can stumble onto a new skill from time to time, deep learning only arrives by design. True and lasting learning of core concepts like force and motion or the causes of war, as well as skills like reading and writing, requires explicit instruction and purposeful practice. There is no way around it.

In fact, Dewey would say that school should always be forward-thinking in giving students what they need now and down the road. In many of his writings, he pleaded for lessons designed to build student practice in solving problems so they could tackle the future challenges they would face. "Wholly independent of desire or intent, every experience lives on in future experiences. Hence the central problem of an education based on experience is to select the kind of present experiences that live fruitfully and creatively in subsequent experiences" (Dewey (1938) 2015, 27–8). If we accept this premise as a key tenet of schooling, then the most important lessons we create are not just explicit and skill based. They are also applied and transferable. Let's be clear that schooling is most impactful when it is both explicit and applied, not one or the other.

Because students arrive at school with a variety of skills, teachers can get disheartened quickly when they observe some students learning while others are falling way behind. Despite our best attempts, we are frustrated, we are out of ideas, and we are running out of patience. The good news is there are strategies that we have not yet tried. There are still a few tricks up our sleeves because learning is never lucky. It doesn't arrive by accident.

The Surefire Techniques That Impact Learning

Every teacher has a favorite strategy, which might be better described as a favorite "teacher trick" or "teacher move" to get students' attention, maintain classroom order, elicit better responses, and increase student skills. With more than three million public school teachers in the United States alone, there are a lot of favorite ideas out there to consider (National Center for Education Statistics 2023). Not to mention that many of our preferred strategies have been modified by teachers across thousands of classrooms so that makes it difficult for educators to even agree on the names and definitions of the techniques we're describing. As just one example, a popular discussion protocol like think-pair-share has dozens of variations and someone might even have a different name for it.

Selecting any technique as better than another does not come without debate, and that is a good thing. The ongoing professional discussion about what works best in school remains a healthy exercise, and it is one that we have been having for a long time. Philosophical debates about the best way to teach and learn have been going on since ancient times. Much of what we know about good instruction today began with philosophers like Aristotle and Socrates, who taught without whiteboards and touch screens in case you didn't know. Many consider Aristotle to be the world's first expert in teaching, and some claim that everything we do in schools today can be traced to him.

With all due respect to the ancients, we have advanced as an industry in the way we train our teachers and teach our kids. We have learned a great deal about effective pedagogy, in large part because our basic mission has never shifted, transferring absolute knowledge and wisdom from adults to children. To be sure, our teaching techniques are more engaging and effective now than they have ever been. Student collaboration and applied learning have advanced significantly, and our classroom cultures are more inclusive and supportive. Though we have made significant strides, we still find some students in every school who are thriving and some who are not. Across our industry, we have not yet solved the crisis of confidence.

What we know for certain through years of practice, observation, and research is that some things we do as teachers work better to advance learning than others. Just as we have learned what works, we have learned what does not. Most alarming is that some things we do in our classrooms actually hinder learning. For example, we know that boredom or disinterest (which we control) diminishes learning, as does ridicule and sarcasm (which we control), along with system decisions like student retention (also under our control). On the contrary, we know that positive teacher-student relationships (which we control) and the use of learning scaffolds (which we control) enhance learning. We know this not because there was one study, one time, in one school in the middle of nowhere. We know it because we have hundreds of studies and classroom observations across countless schools and districts.

With so much rich history to rely on and easy access to quality research studies, we can find summary evidence to support the best ideas to improve education. To be clear, the most reliable source for what works in schools is still the great teacher down the hallway. Observing them in action can provide specific and repeatable best practices. Though much can be gained from reviewing the results of one study or one school, the focus of this chapter is on the critical levers that work across schools in an attempt to isolate the no-doubt-about-it winners for impacting learning in any classroom.

Finalizing any list is inherently a subjective exercise but can be helpful in focusing the conversation among colleagues. It is important to have honest dialogue about what really works in schools because the wave of new teachers entering our profession comes with a tsunami of advice from fellow teachers and administrators about what works best. If we don't navigate these discussions properly, our new teachers may be convinced that many things work equally well and that they are equally important, from how we hand out papers to the objectives we write on the board. This is frustrating for teachers who are trying to sort out what to rely on the most. While it is true that many things positively impact achievement, there are some that stand above the rest and must be part of every teacher's repertoire.

It is important to note that the five levers provided in this chapter are specific to mastering academic content. While there are many techniques used to build classroom community (e.g., knowing each student's name), the focus here is on isolating the actions that lead directly to the acquisition of core content knowledge and skills. We can all agree that having positive classroom conditions is important, but it may be best to view those actions as prerequisites for learning. For now, we will think of them as required preconditions (e.g., safety, culture, and climate) that must be in place for any lesson to work. They are not causing learning to occur, but they can unravel it before it begins. If those preconditions are not established, the classroom levers presented in this chapter will fail. To put it bluntly, if students are throwing chairs across the room, it does not matter what learning methods a teacher is trying to employ. With respect to this critical reality, we will address classroom culture in subsequent chapters.

Sorting Through the Research

The art and science of teaching has been reviewed and verified by legitimate studies across every type of school and district. A quick online search can locate a study to affirm or refute any instructional strategy. This is important to consider because we can sometimes talk ourselves into doing things that we enjoy but that are not consistent with best practice. The good news is that we have reliable meta-analyses from distinguished researchers (e.g., Hattie, Marzano) who have made our work easier by isolating the strategies that have the biggest impact on learning. While we can debate these findings, we should not discount them and write them off as scholarly goobly gook. Any quality meta-analysis has something to offer us as practitioners because it reviews the results from many studies and then captures the average or "typical" impact that a particular strategy or intervention has versus another.

Across our industry, the researchers who conduct these substantive analyses are well known and have become synonymous with their findings. Renowned scholars like John Hattie and Robert Marzano are among the most revered and debated. Their research continues to stir discussion in part because any attempt to make a list of what works is going to be scrutinized. Their research methods also come with some skepticism because they assign an effect size (i.e., the degree of impact) to each classroom strategy, action, or intervention that is being studied and sorts them from top to bottom. Of course, reducing any strategy to a number is troubling for many educators who view our profession as both an art and a science. Still, the effective sizes provide a metric for us to weigh and consider, along with reliable observational data and professional logic. A very brief explanation of statistics is needed regarding effect sizes.

Essentially, an effect size is a type of measurement (a number) that expresses in standard deviation units the increase or decrease in measurable achievement (positive or negative) for a group of students who are exposed to a strategy (variable) being studied. Simply put, an effect size of zero means that the strategy had no statistical impact on learning. It neither positively nor negatively affected students in their learning of the material. In turn, strategies with effect sizes above zero were shown to have positive impacts and those below zero had negative impacts. In this manner, the research attempts to pinpoint the degree of impact along a number line from least impactful to most impactful. An effect size at .40 or above is generally viewed as having a meaningful impact on learning (Hattie 2009). In keeping with our number line analogy, effect sizes of 1.0 (one standard deviation above the norm) are particularly impactful, producing an average improvement on student achievement of at least 34 percent. Those variables that are studied and plotted well below the norm have shown less impact and might be described as detrimental to learning. No matter our personal preferences, the strategies showing the highest positive effects across multiple studies are powerful practices that we need to discuss and consider adding to our repertoire.

Any substantive discussion of research findings from the social sciences (e.g., education) comes with a few cautions. Those include generalizing the findings from a study of a few schools to all schools as there are so many variables in play that impact learning, as well as any conclusions that oversimplify the skills and actions of a great teacher. In the end, studying how children learn is never as reliable and definitive as testing the amount of water and sun needed for a plant to grow. Despite these limitations, educational research gives us a peek inside classrooms across a broad landscape and provides insights into what different teachers have tried across communities. In this way, the research provides a trusted source for launching a discussion about what works in schools.

As a starting point, we will use Hattie's work to isolate some of the best strategies. His seminal findings were published in his now-famous book *Visible Learning* and his ranking of more than 200 influences on student

Table 2.1 Structural Versus Instructional Factors That Impact Learning

Structural Examples	Instructional Examples
• Reducing Class Size 0.21 • Summer School 0.23 • Mentoring 0.12 • School Choice Programs 0.12 • Modified School Calendars 0.09 • Teacher Performance Pay 0.05 • Retention (holding students back) -0.32	• Classroom Discussion 0.82 • Summarization 0.79 • Rehearsal and memorization 0.73 • Feedback 0.70 • Spaced vs. massed practice 0.60 • Note-taking 0.50 • Questioning 0.48

Note: Effect size calculated using Cohen's d.
Source: Hattie, John. 2009. Visible Learning: A Synthesis of over 800 Meta-Analyses Relating to Achievement. Routledge.

achievement are fascinating to consider (Hattie 2009). The table below is just a sampling of Hattie's findings, sorted by what we will call structural vs. instructional factors. Structural factors include things like bell schedules, promotion and retention policies, teacher planning time, and class size. Instructional factors are specific classroom actions that are under a teacher's control, from how they ask questions to whether they assign homework. Instructional factors also include strategies like cooperative learning, teacher lecture, formative assessment, and technology integration.

We know intuitively that there is nothing good or bad about a singular strategy or intervention, but we also know that the things we do in class as part of our lesson design and delivery cannot be equally effective. We know as well that implementation matters. Something may be effective in one school because the teacher(s) executed the strategy particularly well, while a sloppy attempt at another school failed miserably. This is why summarizing the findings from multiple studies (meta-analysis) can provide a higher degree of confidence in the outcomes. Determining the good techniques from the very good is critical to our professional learning. In statistical terms, a positive effect size of .40 or above is good but has only a moderate impact on learning, while an effect size of .80 or above is better and has a much larger impact.

The summary research from Hattie and others provides us with reliable strategies within a teacher's control that impact learning across all settings. In most cases, they are all good techniques and very few are harmful to learning. The key for us is to make sure we are doing the most effective ones well, even if there is not much time for anything else. While the high-impact levers provided in this chapter are in alignment with published effect sizes (evidence-based), they are also congruent with observed teacher practices (observation-based). It is only when research and experience are aligned that best practices are affirmed.

In reviewing any research, a key consideration to ponder is this one: Correlation is not causation. Even when a strategy is positively associated with good teaching, the research does not suggest that the strategy is causing learning to happen. For instance, we know that being friendly to students is correlated to positive learning outcomes, but being friendly does not directly lead to learning. Being a nice teacher is a correlation, not a causation. Putting this another way, we know that posting the day's lesson and agenda on the board is good practice, but the reality is that learning can occur in the absence of such things (Scriven 2002, 47–57). In fact, Marzano stopped using the phrase "high yield" because even the strategies that he identified as most effective impact learning only some of the time (Marzano 2009, 30–7). The "yield" or return on investment for using best practices is always positive but can be moderate and is oftentimes situational. Hattie himself cautions us that "if common sense is the litmus test then everything could be claimed to work" (Hattie 2009, 3).

The great news for our profession is that study after study has validated without question the enormous impact that teachers have on learning. The studies have affirmed what we knew all along: teachers influence learning more than other factors and that what happens inside the classroom has greater impact on achievement than things outside of it like before—and after—school programs, summer school, and tutoring (Sanders and Rivers 1996; Hattie 2009). When it comes to student performance on reading and math tests, teachers are estimated to have two to three times the effect on achievement in comparison to other school factors like school facilities and even leadership (Opper 2019). Both research and experience are in sync on this point; it is one of the few indisputable findings in education. The most critical factor to student achievement is not the principal. It is not class size nor the seating arrangements. It is the teacher, and it matters greatly how they design their lessons. In fact, study after study has shown that while factors like poverty and trauma negatively impact learning, great teachers can even overcome those challenges (Sanders and Rivers 1996).

It only makes sense that a teacher's skill and confidence is the number one indicator of whether a child will learn. More than that, it is logical to deduce that a school or grade level with an entire team of highly skilled and confident teachers working together is the most impactful of all possible school factors. Hattie refers to this as "collective teacher efficacy" and it has the highest effect size on his list (1.44). Hattie puts it this way: "It's not just growth mindset. It's not just rah-rah thinking. It's not just, 'Oh, we can make a difference.' But it's that combined belief that it's us that causes the learning. It's not the students" (Hattie 2017).

Hattie is not alone. Study after study has affirmed similar results about what works in schools and other researchers have provided their own lists of strategies (e.g., Marzano, Rosenshine). Marzano's first book *Classroom Instruction That Works* provides nine research-based strategies that are highly correlated with student learning (Marzano et al. 2001). Marzano's follow-up books and commentaries have clarified some of his early research, though his original list of strategies remain highly relevant and effective.

Rosenshine summarized his groundbreaking research in a series of articles that narrowed the most effective teacher actions down to ten (Rosenshine 2012, 12–19). Rosenshine's approach focused on observing the actions of master teachers, as well as a substantive review of the findings from cognitive science. He subscribed to the notion that direct teacher instruction, along with requisite student practice was most effective. He found that "the most successful teachers spent more time in guided practice, more time asking questions, more time checking for understanding, and more time correcting errors" (Rosenshine 2012, 17). The summary table provided identifies the key classroom actions from each of these renowned researchers that are common or similar, such as summarizing, note-taking, discussion, practice, and feedback. Without a doubt, these are best practices.

In search of the most common practices that work across different schools and classrooms, very few meet the standard of being universally supported by researchers and practitioners alike. This is complicated by research limitations in education that are well-noted, including small samples sizes that result from studying one school, and the lack of large-scale longitudinal studies across the industry (Reynolds et al. 2014). It should be noted that the research related to high-impact strategies and routines falls under two categories: *teacher effectiveness research* that focuses on teacher influences on achievement and *educational effectiveness research* that considers broader factors like school improvement and leadership.

When educators consider and debate evidence-based practices, some of the responses are structural (teacher planning time), some are curricular (access to rigorous texts), and a few of the most powerful are instructional

Table 2.2 Teacher Dilemma: New and Not Confident

Inside the Classroom: A Closer Look
• In a middle school classroom, Ms. Sampson has just been hired to teach a reading intervention class for struggling seventh graders. The class is small, and the students are not much interested in being there. They are fully aware of their struggles and do not want yet another reading class taking up space in their schedules. Ms. Sampson has completed her internship but has never had the responsibility of running her own classroom. She is eager, energetic, and well-read. She studies hard and continues to take all the training that her school offers. Ms. Sampson has been told that her students need to read more rigorous texts, though their reading skills are at least two grade levels below their peers. She has also been told that good classroom routines include student collaboration, movement, and lots of discussion. She jumps right in and does her best to create a learning environment that matches those expectations, only to find that there is a great deal of chaos happening around her, too many students are off task, and most are not improving as readers and thinkers. The teacher does not want to admit that she is not sure where to focus, and she is getting more and more frustrated. She is kind and smart, but she lacks confidence and doesn't want anyone to know.
Considerations and Solutions • Ms. Sampson is not unlike most new teachers. In fact, she is fully credentialed and shows great potential. She simply lacks experience. Her students are not learning as a result. In truth, Ms. Sampson may not make it through the school year. She will almost certainly quit if nothing changes. An assistant principal assigned to support and evaluate Ms. Sampson has already met with her and given her several areas to improve. This has added to the teacher's anxiety, and she does not know which things are most critical for her success, let alone how to fix them. • **In supporting a new teacher**, there are two challenges that must be addressed at the same time, helping them improve their skills and supporting the students so they don't fall behind. Let's be clear that the students must learn at all costs. They are priority number one because a school cannot let another year pass without these students improving their skills dramatically as readers. We also don't want to undermine Ms. Sampson to the degree that she loses even more confidence and gives up. A possible solution is narrowing the teacher's focus to one or two actions that will help the students learn, and that are relatively easy for a new teacher to implement. The goal here is for the students to learn and grow, and for the teacher to gain confidence that she is making an impact. In this class, the teacher might focus on (i) Modeling good reading and thinking habits for students as a whole class exercise and then (ii) Providing practice time by giving students a simple but meaningful assignment to work on in pairs. Having students read and discuss in pairs will be more manageable for the teacher than organizing larger student groups. These steps will also limit movement in the classroom and help her regain some order to the chaos. Training and coaching support for Ms. Sampson should be limited to the steps she can handle and that will make the most difference for learning.

(Continued)

Table 2.2 *(Cont.)*

Inside the Classroom: A Closer Look
• **A caution for school leaders** is resisting the temptation to give up on Ms. Sampson. It is not fair to compare her to veteran teachers or even to the superstar new teacher down the hallway. We should also be cautious in expecting improvement in too many areas. It is best to provide coaching on the teacher's craft, not just process improvements. Yes, she should stand at her door and greet her students. Yes, she should have a clean classroom, take attendance efficiently, attend PLCs, etc. Still, most of those things will not impact her students' reading struggles this year. If Ms. Sampson does not gain confidence in sound pedagogy, the students will not gain confidence as readers. It should be noted that schools sometimes give up on struggling teachers only to find that there are no other replacements ready to step in. If we give up on Ms. Sampson, we may be right back in the same place this summer, hiring another new teacher and starting over again.

(learning and engagement strategies). To be clear, the focus here is on the instructional methods and techniques that any teacher can utilize, and that all schools should invest in. In drawing a comparison to course standards, it is fair to say that most educators agree that there are essential topics and skills (the critical curriculum) that must be taught in schools, while acknowledging that there are other things we can teach kids that are nice-to-know but not as important. In the same way, these levers are provided as the most important classroom actions (the essential pedagogy) that we must get right, while admitting that there are many great strategies and techniques that are nice to use but not essential.

While the levers presented are few in number, each one requires a great deal of skill and practice for teachers to master and use properly. As an example, we know that just because there is academic discourse evident in a classroom doesn't mean that it is impacting learning. As well, just because students are taking notes doesn't mean they are benefitting from it. Though there are powerful methods for giving students feedback, there are less effective ones. To increase student achievement without fail, we must execute these levers at the highest levels, for each one of them gives life to learning. They are oxygen.

No matter what else is on our plates as educators, we must get professional development right because mastery of the teacher's craft is the most important ingredient in eliminating achievement gaps and realizing academic success for all. The five learning levers that are most important in mastering academic content are explained in this chapter. They are presented visually (see Figure 2.1) at the bottom of triangle to highlight their importance

Table 2.3 Summary of Hattie, Marzano, and Rosenshine Methods That Impact Learning

Hattie	Marzano	Rosenshine
• Cognitive task analysis. • Strategies to integrate with prior knowledge. • Transfer strategies. • Classroom discussion. • Summarization. • Deliberate practice. Spaced practice. • Evaluation and reflection. • Reciprocal teaching. • Scaffolding. • Planning and Prediction. • Feedback.	• Identifying similarities and differences. • Summarizing and note taking. • Reinforcing effort and providing recognition. • Homework and practice. • Non-linguistic representations. • Cooperative learning. • Setting objectives and providing feedback. • Generating and testing hypotheses. • Cues, questions, and advance organizers	• Reviewing previous learning. • Presenting new material in small steps. • Questioning and checks for understanding. • Teacher think aloud and modeling. • Guided student practice. • Scaffolds for difficult tasks. • Providing systematic feedback and corrections. • Requiring and monitoring independent practice. • Engaging students in weekly and monthly reviews. • Re-teaching when necessary.

Sources: Hattie, John. 2009. *Visible Learning: A Synthesis of over 800 Meta-Analyses Relating to Achievement*. Routledge; Marzano, Robert, Pickering, Debra, and Pollock, Jane. 2001. *Classroom Instruction That Works: Research-Based Strategies for Increasing Student Achievement*. Association for Supervision and Curriculum Development; Rosenshine, Barak. 2012. "Principles of Instruction. Research-Based Strategies That All Teachers Should Know." *American Educator* Spring 2012: 12–19.

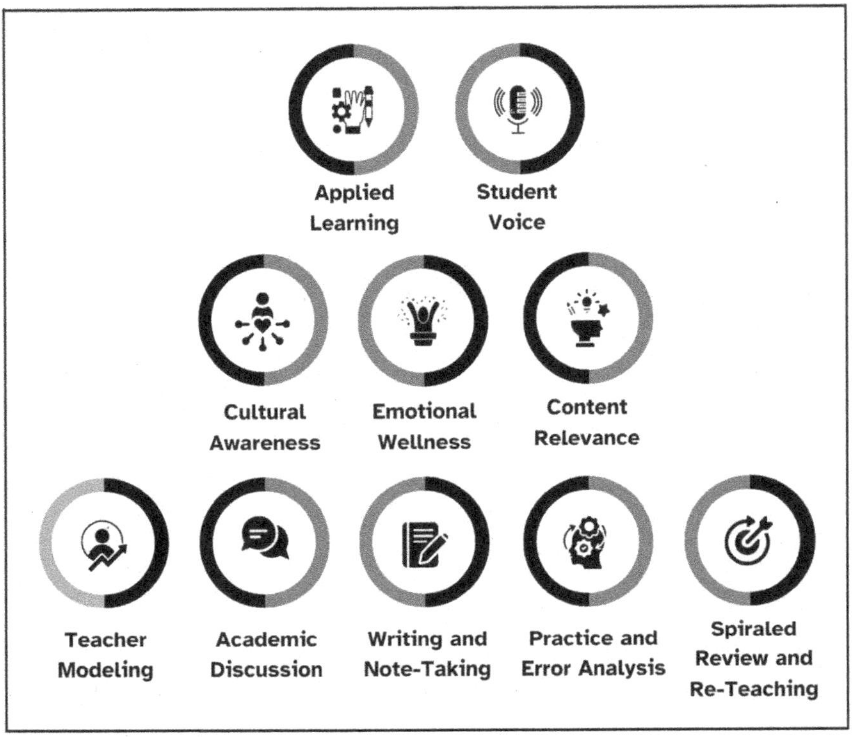

Figure 2.1 *High impact learning levers triangle diagram.*

as foundational. The remaining levers that impact student engagement are addressed in the upcoming chapters.

The Art of Lifting Heavy Things

It is not far-fetched to suggest that getting students to learn something in the face of so many obstacles is akin to pushing what seems to be an immovable object up a steep mountain. Even among our best teachers, this can lead to some stressful and exhausting days, endless frustrations and headaches, and almost always a bad back. It might be best to conjure up a picture of some ancient warriors pushing a stone armory uphill and into battle. The good news is that the ancients taught us a lot about winning battles. They showed us long ago that we can move really heavy things if we have the will to do so and some seriously good tools. The invention and use of pulleys and levers was a marvel of ancient technology and made impossible tasks possible, and the building of great things manageable.

Yes, it is true that we could move the world if we had a lever long enough (thank you, Archimedes). We know that levers come in all shapes and sizes, and they help us to move and lift heavy things. In military parlance, levers are both physical tools and strategic maneuvers that are sometimes described as "force multipliers." These are actions that allow someone to accomplish greater feats than they can without them. As an example, it makes sense that drones can be deployed in creating more surgical strikes against an enemy target than one would expect from sending in hundreds of troops marching in formation. We could also say that computers and robotics have created more efficient functions that were simply not possible when everything was done by hand. We have also seen the impact of an inspiring leader who rallies an organization to great success even in places where outcomes have been stagnant for years. Yes, people can be force multipliers as well.

With this in mind, any credible summary of instructional best practices should include methods that are both necessary for student learning and that accelerate achievement in a way that can be described as force multipliers. To that end, it is hard to consider a strategy or technique as mission critical if it does not meet the following conditions: (i) That learning cannot occur or is hindered if the strategy is not in place, and (ii) That learning is reliably assured or accelerated if the strategy is properly implemented. Let's apply that two-part test to better understand our assessment of best practices:

- *Is the use of graphic organizers in a classroom helpful to student learning?* YES
    - *Can learning occur without the use of graphic organizers?* YES
- *Is the use of error analysis in a classroom helpful in student learning?* YES
    - *Can learning occur in the absence of error analysis?* NO

While graphic organizers are helpful but optional, error analysis is a vital and integral method to drive learning. Decisions like these about what works best are made easier when theory, research, and practice are in alignment. The learning levers discussed below meet any threshold for effectiveness and impact. It should be noted that none of them are groundbreaking, and all are familiar to us. They are evidence-based, logical, and practical. They are equally important, mutually reliant, and (no) they are not optional.

Teacher Modeling / High Expectations

The idea of setting high expectations in our classrooms is more than simply believing that all children can learn. It is expecting that all children will learn and then creating the classroom conditions for getting them there. That begins by ensuring that students know what success looks like. Let's be clear about this: All students can achieve at grade level, but they will not learn if they are unclear about what they are supposed to be learning. In fact, this concept is so critical that students can oftentimes learn just by showing them what is expected. Whether we use the term "learning target," "success criteria," or something else, students must have a clear and explicit understanding of what they are striving for, along with examples of what it looks like to reach mastery.

It is important to note that all students want to achieve. It is part of our human nature to seek out learning, which is probably related to our survival instincts (and to Aristotle, of course). It is clear from the dawn of time that human beings want to be smart and skilled, even if we say or act otherwise. In other words, we are created intrinsically motivated so the simple act of showing students what high expectations look like is a gigantic step in building their confidence. Though it is true that some students lack motivation, it is important to note that they did not start out that way and their disinterest in learning is often short-lived and always reversible.

Modeling expectations for students usually comes in two forms: (i) providing worked examples or exemplars that are available for students to review and (ii) modeling our own thinking and skills as teachers that students can mimic moving forward. Setting high expectations in a classroom might sound something like this:

- *"Students, we are going to learn this new dance routine so let's all gather around and I'll show what it looks like when it is done perfectly."*
- *"Students, we are going to learn how to infer meaning from complex political cartoons so let's look at a really hard one, and we'll make sense of it together."*
- *"Students, we going to learn to use power verbs to improve our writing so let's take a look at a great piece of prose and see if we can push ourselves to write like this."*

There are simply no shortcuts to true learning. If we want students to dance perfectly, we must model perfect dancing. It is illogical to show them a dance routine done poorly, unless our purpose is for them to compare bad dancing with good dancing. It is best to think of this modeling approach as backwards design or teaching with the end in mind that is most effective when we provide students with clear success criteria. When we get it right, we might be surprised to hear reactions that sound something like this: *"Oh, you want me to do that? Ok. I got it now. I may need to practice a few times, but I can do that."*

- **Classroom Examples:**
  - **Writing / Presentations.** If a student is going to be a great writer, the teacher and students have to agree first and foremost what great writing looks like. Even if we differ a little per our own perceptions, we can at least determine a lousy piece of writing from a middling one, and we can certainly distinguish a just-good-enough, middle-of-the-road attempt from a powerful, breathtaking paper or poem that is penned by a famous author or by a young student. Let's consider a young writer in middle school who is proud of her essay and is a little frustrated that she received a B grade from her teacher. According to her teacher, the student's writing at this moment is good but not excellent.

    In the student's mind, she worked hard and was convinced she deserved the highest praise possible. In the teacher's mind, she knows that holding the young writer to the standard will push her to excel and that the teacher's expectations for the student were higher than her expectations of herself. The key here is to motivate the student, not by grades, but by believing she can do better and giving her honest feedback. Writing is an easy example because there are countless examples of great writing that a teacher can use as models. In this example, effective instruction begins with showing students those examples and then simply asking them: "Now that you've completed your assignment, let's compare your draft to our exemplars and see how close you are."

    Students sometimes appear to be content with mediocrity, and teachers can sometimes resist pushing them harder as a way of avoiding conflict. When we do this, we send a message that we are okay with less-than-expected outcomes. This type of deficit thinking is rarely seen when we observe our best teachers in action. Feedback to students can come across as biting and hurtful if we don't get it right but can be messaged as constructive and caring in the hands of a great teacher. "This is good, but this over here is even better. Let's work together to get you there." If done well, setting high expectations for students should not lead to frustration but a sense of fulfillment and pride.

- **Projects / Labs.** The same high expectations can be applied to any classroom assignment such as a culminating project or lab activity. A teacher's expectations of projects and labs should be very high and using exemplars designed by students can work well in setting success criteria. We should be clear here that utilizing projects as evidence of learning are highly suspect if the assignment and expectations are not clear and-or not tied a standard. We have all seen projects that are pretty to look at but do not showcase learning. More often than not, these types of projects do more to limit learning than they do to advance it. We also know that projects that are completed at home (oftentimes with the assistance of a parent or guardian) can create inequity as students do not have access to similar resources or even a quiet place to work. With that noted, projects and labs completed at school can provide quality hands-on learning opportunities if they are properly planned and scaffolded. Students can benefit by showcasing their learning and by practicing their fine motor skills, creativity, and attention to detail.

  Some examples for teachers to consider are the high-quality history fair projects and science fair boards that showcase student research and findings. Some of these include a properly cited process paper, pictures of student experiments in action, and deep synthesis of the student's research questions and answers. Once again, students should be provided with models of excellent projects and be held to that standard. A mistake teachers make sometimes is giving students a rubric with no model and then simply collecting the assignment a few days later and offering up a grade. A better approach is a developmental one that guides the student to mastery. In this scenario, the teacher would check in on the projects while they are under construction so that every project is excellent when finished. The goal of any assignment is to scaffold learning in such a way that everyone learns, and everyone is proud of their work. The students have seen success and gained confidence because they took on something and perfected it, not because they tried hard and came up short. They have nailed it, and they know it. And, yes, in this example, everyone gets an A.

Academic success goes much further than simply telling our students that we believe in them and then hoping they are successful. There are many strategies and tools associated with modeling high expectations, as long as they have the purpose of getting all students to mastery. A key step in building confidence is believing that all children can meet grade-level standards, putting into action the processes that help students know what the standards are, ensuring that they know how close they are to meeting them, and giving them the tools and scaffolds to get there. Like any great technique, this requires purposeful planning and precise execution.

Teacher Modeling / Strategies to Consider:

- Think Aloud
- Worked Examples / Exemplars
- Scaffolds / Anchor charts
- Rubrics / Success Criteria
- Criteria for Credit
- Criteria for Quality
- No Opt Out

Academic Discussion / Questioning

When students talk about what they are learning, they learn more. There is simply no disputing this fact. Come to think of it, it is sad to ponder about how many years we tried to get students to stop talking in class. Talking to others, and to ourselves, about grade-level content helps us to process and synthesize our learning and then attach it to long-term memory. Though students can learn without discussion, their learning is ripened and hardened by collaborating with others. In fact, it is not a stretch to say that we have not learned something until we have talked about it. It might be best to view discussion as verbalizing our cognitive reasoning.

We should be reminded that for most of human history (which pre-dates the written word), learning was derived by watching and doing (apprenticeship) and by listening to and following others (mentorship). In ancient times, the process began with modeling (watch me and do what I do) and was followed by discussion (tell me what you think about that). *"Let me show you how to hunt a deer"* (modeling). *"Tell me why you think the world is round"* (discussion). As we all know, the Socratic method remains one of the most powerful ways of developing deep thinking, whether students are discussing civics or science or their favorite music. There is little room for debate in research and practice about the importance of questioning and discussion because we know that talking about content cements learning more effectively than just hearing about it or reading about it.

The good news is that we see more discussion in our classrooms than ever before, and all teachers have their favorite strategies and protocols for students to talk about content. As mentioned, the strategy is less important than the approach. The key to success with any good discussion protocol is giving students time to talk as a processing step, including honest reflections about what they don't understand. Simply going through the motions of a discussion protocol is not enough and does not lead to learning. The protocol simply provides a ripe time and space where learning might occur. This is where the teacher steps in to ensure that the pacing of the strategy is right, and that the discussion is productive.

This is a good time to remind us that school is about meeting student needs, not our own. As teachers, we can sometimes convince ourselves that we did everything correctly, that we gave the students the right activities and good directions. Then, when some students don't know the material, we turn our frustrations on them. They could have done more. They could have worked harder and listened better. This is where the art of teaching comes in, where subtle maneuvers and nuance mean a great deal in whether students learn or not. A key instructional observer can spot the difference between a novice teacher who uses a strategy but does not get good results versus a master teacher who uses the same strategy with a little bit of tweaking and sees dramatic achievement. Success typically arrives when there is good pacing to the discussion, and clear intent as to what students should be talking about.

In the hands of our best teachers, discussion techniques include posing the right questions, providing the right amount of time for students to dialogue, and ensuring the right degrees of participation from each child. No matter what, some student discussion is better than no discussion. It may be hard to hear this, but teachers sometimes get caught up in listening to their own voices via lectures, stories, and slide presentations. In doing so, they lose sight of the fact that the one who is talking the most is the one who is learning the most. Socrates himself was one of the most brilliant thinkers ever to live, and even he knew how important it was to speak less, to ask great questions, to get his students talking, and to not answer the questions for them.

As teachers learn the best methods for academic discourse, it is a good idea to consider a few questions regarding purpose and pacing. Is this a good time in the lesson for students to stop and discuss? What are the students supposed to be talking about? How long should this discussion go on? How might students report out? Remember that learning is the only true outcome of any discussion protocol. If the students didn't learn, the activity and directions we gave them were not sufficient, and only we can change that.

- **Classroom Example:**
  - **Whole Class Discussion.** Though some elements of a lesson can lend themselves to discussion better than others, rich and powerful student discourse can occur in pairs, small groups, or with an entire class. In this example, the teacher is not fully comfortable with putting students in groups nor with allowing too much movement in the classroom. While keeping the class as a large group, the teacher can still begin the lesson by posing a challenging question or dilemma for students to consider. This is a good way for students to be engaged and talking right from the start of class, even before proceeding with direct instruction. To ensure that all students have something to discuss, the teacher gives them a few minutes to jot down their thoughts. At this point, the teacher can certainly lead a healthy whole-group discussion, connecting the question that was posed to today's lesson and, quite possibly, learning a few things about what the students know and don't know. This teacher can keep the class seated as a whole group and still ask students to talk to someone next to them or just read what they have written down. The key here for the teacher is to call on just enough students to get the whole-class discussion started, and that the discussion doesn't go on too long and distract or delay the lesson itself. In this example, the discussion must connect to the lesson in some way. If the two are unrelated, the students might find the discussion interesting but it will not impact learning. Of course, a short and effective discussion protocol can be planned for anytime during the lesson. The students can be provided with a very brief moment for a turn-and-talk or table-talk discussion

so they can reveal their current reasonings and misunderstandings during or after the teacher's direct instruction segment. This is a great opportunity for students to use their newly acquired content vocabulary, and (if done well) to discuss their learning in a safe space without fear of ridicule and being wrong.

An important point to mention is that teachers should allow students to talk freely but not to allow misunderstandings to linger. Just as discussion cements learning, it can also cement not learning. If a student utters a misunderstanding to a classmate, there is a very real chance that each student involved in the dialogue may believe the response to be correct. This is why conversation among students in pairs or small groups is best when it includes a mechanism for students to record and share out what they heard, and for the teacher to correct misinterpretations on the spot. While every lesson is different, a few suggestions are provided here to ensure that the discussion is in keeping with best practice: Classroom discussion (whole group or student-to-student) must have a direct academic purpose; Academic talk must require all students (not the same students) to contribute; Students should be asked to use content vocabulary to explain their thinking; Teachers should be highly attentive to student responses with the purpose of correcting misunderstandings and building community.

Academic Discourse / Strategies to Consider:

- Think-Pair-Share
- Defend Your Answer
- Fishbowl
- Four Corners
- Gallery Walk / Carousel Graffiti
- Concentric Circles
- Pinwheel

Writing / Note-Taking

Like discussion, writing is a critical exercise in deepening student learning. As any adult will tell you, we tend to remember things better when we write them down. When students talk about content, they are more likely to learn it. When they write about content, they are more likely to recall it. Writing is so universally important that if students did nothing else but write a summary at the end of every lesson or unit, they would learn a great deal more than if they did not. Neurobiologists have affirmed that writing activates all parts of the brain and helps form sequences to help us shape random things into patterns that help us remember them (Marzano et al. 2001). This conjures up memories of sitting in a quiet room somewhere taking a test and recalling the right answers simply by picturing in our minds the exact location in our notes where the information was written down.

In Marzano's list of the nine strategies that most impact student achievement, summarizing and note-taking are presented side-by-side as the most useful types of writing for learning (Marzano et al. 2001). While any form of writing is helpful, summarizing and note-taking are particularly effective because they require the learner to sort through large amounts of information and synthesize the most important things to remember. This requires students to think by substituting, deleting, and keeping some things (Marzano et al. 2001). The critical attribute in utilizing high-impact summary strategies is the analytical skill required of the students in completing the task (Rosenshine et al. 1996, 181–221).

The simple act of asking students to summarize their learning and pinpoint areas of confusion is an easy-to-implement assignment in any classroom. The trick here is for teachers to mix up the types of writing assignments to keep students engaged and to provide the right amount of time for students to capture their thinking without taking time away from other important activities. This is where proper planning and execution of student discussion and writing protocols converge. Pacing and purpose are key. As such, we must pay constant attention to the students sitting in front of us to determine if more or less time is needed.

In classrooms where all students learn, time is never wasted. Adjusting the timing and purpose of an activity just a little bit can enhance learning without losing instructional time. In observations of our best teachers, we often see them pivot when they sense they are talking too long and move into a short protocol by asking students to pair up and discuss something they learned today or that still confuses them. The students are asked to jot down their thoughts and share them with a classmate for a minute or two. The teacher can then randomize who to call on and how long the debrief should proceed. While these techniques are skillfully utilized in the hands of a master teacher, a novice teacher may allow the writing, discussion, and debrief to go on far too long, even to the point that students are off task and frustrated.

Of course, there are dozens of great strategies for students to capture their thinking through writing, and some are more manageable than others. The key to any successful writing activity is tied to its intended outcome. Asking students to write a few bulleted items on a sticky note or compose a five-paragraph essay can both be effective (or not) if the teacher outlines a clear purpose and if students understand and value that purpose. For instance, if a teacher asks students to fill out a learning journal everyday with no purpose, it may lead to students resenting the activity and, even worse, resenting writing. Teachers should always utilize the quickest and most effective formats for students to capture their thinking and summarize information, keeping in mind how critical the information is for students to learn and the best ways to help students load that information into long-term memory. This is why short summaries and note-taking of any type are considered the most effective and efficient.

- **Classroom Example:**
  - **Writing Across the Subject Areas.** Writing of any format across any subject or topic tends to accomplish two things: (i) It requires students to reflect upon and synthesize what they have learned and-or (ii) It allows students an opportunity to extend their learning to related topics beyond the current lesson. In either case, the trick for teachers is figuring out how to review and-or grade all that writing. It is logical to suggest that students will do their best work when they think the teacher is going to read it. There are many ways to address this, including reading and remarking on student writing without grading it. As just one example, students can complete several writing assignments before the teacher reviews them. The teacher can then randomly select one or two papers to read and comment on. In this example, the students never know what paper will be selected and possibly graded. The teacher can then use two or three of the best papers from the class for students to review as exemplars (models).

    Teachers often require students to keep their writings in a notebook and then grade them later after asking students to choose two or three that they feel are the best ones. Of course, teachers can make their work more efficient if they read for specific feedback instead of marking up every mistake. A teacher can read for content, for opinions, or for style. As example, a language arts teacher might encourage the class to include more interesting word choices or rhetorical devices and read only for those things. A teacher from another subject area might have challenged the class to include key academic vocabulary terms in their responses and then only reads for the proper use of those words. Feedback and grading depend in large part on teacher preference and the format of the writing itself. As a general rule, short writing assignments rarely need to be graded and feedback on the content is often more important than the quality of the writing. Long-form writing takes a great deal of investment from students and deserves a full review of content and style. It should be noted that creative writing assignments across the subject areas can also be fun ways to engage students, as long as the students see the connection between writing a poem or an extended metaphor and the content they are learning. Expectations around quality are only as good as the amount of feedback that the teacher can provide. Student writing improves through teacher modeling, constructive feedback, and student practice.

Though writing is viewed as a universally effective means to advance learning, it should be noted that artificial intelligence will increasingly make the art and craft of writing less necessary. Speaking, not writing, may become the critical literacy skill for the coming generations. The future of formal writing structures that are commonplace in schools, including essays and poetry, will likely be replaced by artificial intelligence (AI) technology or be augmented to a degree that teachers will not be able to distinguish between original student responses and those that are technology enhanced. Still, short writing assignments that are intended for learning content or recording ideas will continue to have a place in our classrooms as a higher-order learning activity.

Writing and Note-Taking / Strategies to Consider:

- Summary Frames
- Classifying / Outlining
- Extended Metaphor / Analogy
- Concept Mapping / Webbing
- Everybody Writes

- 3-2-1 Protocol
- Gist Protocol

Student Practice / Error Analysis

In the simplest of terms, students cannot learn what they have not practiced. Yes, students might understand something for a moment if asked about it in class but moving that information into long-term memory requires multiple exposures and repeated practice (Ebbinghaus 1913; Zahn et al., 2018, 1–14; Carpenter et al., 2022, 496–511). The idea that students need to practice new skills may seem obvious, but it is easier said than done. As with the other critical levers, the struggle is finding the right time to practice, the right amount of practice, and the best ways to provide feedback. A common concern across schools is finding a proper balance between the amount of practice and the amount of feedback. When we get it wrong, teachers can sometimes give up on the idea entirely because it feels unwieldy and unproductive with so many students to serve.

Practice and feedback routines are key areas for professional development and instructional coaching that get lost in many schools. The classroom strategies that teachers implement are influenced greatly by the training they receive and the feedback they get from the administrators who conduct their evaluations. For example, it is more likely than not that teachers have taken part in school and district training on discussion and writing protocols. The same goes for administrators. It is less common to see professional development in areas like independent practice, small group intervention, and grading. If educators are not fully aware of the best practices in these areas, they can mistakenly see student practice and feedback as lost instructional time. In fact, it is not uncommon to see teachers suddenly switch their instructional plans when a visitor enters the room and sees the students working on something independently. This is a good place to remind us that we do not know if students have learned something until they show us. Student practice is the threshold that we must cross successfully in moving from teaching and presenting something to learning and mastering content. This is a key moment in building student confidence. Teachers must know if each student individually has mastered the required content or skill. In the absence of that assurance, we are just guessing, hoping, and moving on.

A key growth step for teachers is finding a favorite strategy or two for releasing learning in a way that provides students with time for processing and practicing. Journals, miniature white boards, and various technology applications provide engaging tools for students to practice and be held individually accountable for their responses. Practice time in class can be easily coupled with discussion protocols via strategies like turn-and-talk, think-pair-share, and even whole-group debriefs. No matter the methods teachers use to get students to think, practice, and discuss, they are not adequate for ensuring mastery in the absence of a feedback loop. Practice without feedback is inefficient and ineffective.

One of the most elusive practices in education is mastering the art of individual feedback when there are a whole lot of students and only one teacher. There are two suggestions provided here that are commonly observed among top-notch teachers: (i) Student Error Analysis and (ii) Checks for Understanding. These are advanced practices that work in any classroom, though they are not easy to do and are often misapplied in the hands of fledging teachers. Teachers struggle in these areas either by rushing the entire process and-or by checking on student learning without correcting the misconceptions. Rushing through a strategy or protocol can be just as harmful as slowing it down and wasting instructional time. Though checks for understanding are commonly utilized in schools, there is often more checking going on than correcting. Correcting means clarifying or even re-teaching and teachers sometimes skip that part because they have a clock in their heads and time is ticking. Checking understanding is a process for ensuring mastery that must be coupled with correcting understanding. We might refer to this with students as flexing their understanding.

In keeping with best practice, our lessons must include feedback steps that show students explicitly what they got right and what they got wrong (error analysis) and then circle back around to check on their understanding again and again (feedback loops). While this can be exhausting, there are a few tricks that keep the process manageable. As an example, student error analysis can be effective as a whole class exercise just as much as it can with small groups or individual students. A teacher reviewing correct and incorrect responses on a whiteboard for the entire class to view can be done efficiently, especially when coupled with a quick turn-and-talk opportunity for students to discuss where they went wrong. This is where the learning levers presented via this chapter work together to ensure mastery, including teacher modeling (whole group), student discussion (pairs or small group), and error analysis.

So we don't overthink it, let's remember that a whole lot of learning can occur when a teacher simply asks pointed questions and allows students time to ponder and respond: *Why is this answer right and this one wrong? Why is this the best choice among the answers provided? What do you notice about this incorrect answer choice that made so many of you select it?* The key for teachers in this process is not moving too quickly when it appears that many students have mastered the content while some have not. The few who got it wrong must know why and be provided with a chance to relearn the material. Though we like to celebrate incremental growth for students on their paths to proficiency, the end goal is not academic progress. It is mastery. That is why the most meaningful outcome of any type of practice routine is perfection. Whether students are learning how to solve for x or how to throw a curveball, we are most helpful to them when we pinpoint exactly what they are doing wrong and then don't give up until they get it right. Though telling a student we are proud of them for making progress is encouraging, allowing them to not reach proficiency is damaging. In fact, it is common across youth and professional sports for coaches to remind their players that practice does not make perfect. Only perfect practice makes perfect.

- **Classroom Example:**
  - **Multiple Choice Mathematics.** It is an important life lesson for students to grasp that there are right answers and wrong answers, just as there are kind remarks and mean-spirited ones. There are opinions and there are facts. In a world filled with so much information and so many viewpoints, it can sometimes sound like everything is acceptable and that no idea is a bad one. We see this in schools when a student offers up a misinformed comment or turns in a poorly executed assignment. Even if they are proud of their work, somebody must tell them that more revision is required. Yes, it is okay to tell students they are wrong. In fact, it is our moral obligation, as well as a professional hazard. Students, like adults, do not like to be wrong, and there are techniques that our best teachers use in getting the point across in a supportive manner. The most effective methods arise when students come to their own conclusions that their essay or project is not that good, or that their answer is not quite right. In fact, there is a powerful transfer that

occurs from teaching to learning when a student sees something without the teacher telling them.

Some of the most compelling evidence for practice and feedback is found among highly effective math teachers. One top-notch technique that is commonly deployed is providing a set of multiple-choice answers and asking students which answer choice is the most correct. In other words, which response is "absolutely correct," which one is "absolutely wrong," and which is "not correct but close." Which one did I almost select as a student but did not? If executed properly, this activity requires deep reflection and error analysis among students. Teachers can ask students to think through the choices on their own or in pairs / triads / groups. The key here is encouraging student ownership of their own reasoning and allowing them to correct their own thinking (meta-cognition). In making this a routine across subjects and grade levels, teachers would be wise to ask students to analyze what the class chose as the most-selected wrong answer in distinguishing almost-right from really-right and bringing awareness to their own thinking and reasoning.

Error Analysis / Strategies to Consider:

- Checks for Understanding
- Perfect practice / Right is right
- Peer Review / Feedback
- Placemat Protocol
- Stretch It
- Stop and Jot / Report Out
- Mini Whiteboards

Spiraled Review / Re-Teaching

There is no such thing as being proficient at something in the moment. Proficiency only arrives across time and space. We are easily fooled when a student can do something with great command at one point in time but cannot replicate it many weeks or months later. This is true both when learning a skill (e.g., solving two-step equations), a routine (e.g., twirling flags in the color guard), or core content for a standardized assessment (e.g., the Advanced Placement Biology exam). For this reason, we cannot ensure student success with full certainty until we build ongoing review and re-teaching into our lessons. Reviewing previously learned content comes in many forms, from daily bellringers to pop quizzes. Whatever the format, these routines are essential for ensuring mastery for all students and not including them will always produce inequitable outcomes.

The pressures for teachers that arise from curriculum pacing guides and accountability measures have made this process of spiraled review more challenging. Teachers and administrators keep a close eye on the school-year calendar, and they can feel the weeks rushing by in a hurried attempt to cover what feels like too much material in too little time. Ironically, rushing is a detriment to learning. When we avoid opportunities to review previously covered material to keep all students on pace, we are hindering learning for students who need the most help. The trick to making this work is covering new material while folding in older material as seamlessly as possible. We see this technique built into bellringer review activities and parallel assessments as part of our best teachers' routines and practices.

Complicating matters for newer teachers is their reliance on a single assessment or task to determine student mastery that can often lead to false positives. As an example, a common misstep arises when some or all students master something early in the school year and the teacher is convinced that no review or re-teaching is needed prior to the end-of-year assessment. This blind spot is one of the primary obstacles to increasing proficiency and closing achievement gaps. In the absence of providing students with review and reassessment (even via a mini quiz), teachers are left to guess which students are trending toward mastery. Not knowing which students will perform well by the end of the year and which will not is a frustrating reality for teachers and administrators and leads to conversations that sound like this: *I think student x is going to do well on the state test but I'm not so sure about student y. What do you think?* What starts out as a well-meaning data conversation about children and their needs leads to the labeling and rank-ordering of students and a whole lot of guesswork about who knows what.

The only reliable solution for schools is some form of spiraled review, either jointly designed by a subject or grade-level team or left to the teacher to determine. Either way, review is a powerful best practice that can be built into pacing guides or created as a supplemental resource. Spiraled review or spiraled practice is sometimes referred to as "spaced practice" or "distributed practice." Whatever name and definition you prefer is fine as long as students interact with the critical course content over and over again across the school year.

Once again, the secret to proficiency for all students is a combination of critical content and essential pedagogy, not one or the other. This is especially helpful knowing that some students miss many days of school, and others may transfer into and out of schools during the year. Planning for these gaps in instructional time by incorporating review and re-teaching increases the likelihood that all students will engage with and master grade-level standards. In addition to the academic benefits, the routines of practice, review, and re-teaching go a long way in building pride and confidence because students are interacting with content that is familiar and comfortable.

It should be noted that a great partner tool in this work is the use of formative (and sometimes summative) parallel assessment. These assessments are "parallel" because they involve the use of quizzes and tests that cover generally the same material over and over and provide students multiple attempts to show proficiency as well as repeated exposure to the critical content. As an example, let's say a student in middle school has just taken a test over the assigned material in his science class and does not do well. If the goal here is providing the student with a grade and moving on, there is nothing to do. If the goal is content acquisition, the student should be provided with an opportunity to take a similar or "parallel assessment" a few days or weeks later to see if they can improve their results. In some schools, these assessments (if graded) can also be used to improve a student's grade because the second attempt typically allows for improved performance and provides a replacement grade that makes the first attempt null and void. That is why it is common to find schools using parallel assessment when they already utilize some form of standards-based or equitable grading practices. To ensure that students do their best with subsequent test attempts, schools often limit the number of chances to retest (the attempts are not endless) and require students to attend a tutoring session before retesting (there are no free rides).

- **Classroom Example:**
    - **Sort-of Knowing vs Really Knowing.** There are many subjects in school that are content heavy, from fifth grade math to US History to

Chemistry. As teachers know all too well, the units and lessons for any subject are played out across a school-year calendar that offers many days for powerful engagement and learning, along with countless interruptions that arise from things like holiday breaks, schoolwide assemblies, and student absences. These interruptions reduce the opportunities for students to learn by days or weeks and contribute to achievement gaps for those who are more likely to miss school (i.e., students from low socioeconomic households).

In this example, let's say that a teacher of eighth grade science does a great job covering compounds and elements in the fall and may be convinced that her students are well on their way to acing the state science assessment at the end of the year. Of course, as fate would have it, a variety of challenges can and will crop up in the coming weeks. Let's consider a few that could thwart the teacher's plans. (i) While nearly all the students in the class showed deep understanding of the material, two of them missed most of the unit and are completely lost; (ii) Some of the student schedules will shift for second semester and the teacher will get some new students who she didn't teach first semester; (iii) The students will certainly forget some (if not most) of the material that was covered in the fall. The solution here for the teacher involves some combination of reviewing and re-teaching subject matter that she has already taught, even if some students have already mastered it.

A good option is implementing a brief bellringer activity as a spiraled review that includes both new material and previously covered topics. This kind of daily or weekly review can be short (two or three questions), can be graded or not, and can be constructed as a quiz, game, or competition. The key here for the teacher is to pay particular attention to the common mistakes that students are making and then briefly re-teach that material. The teacher must also take notice of the students who are still struggling no matter how many times that material has been covered. Those students must be given one-on-one or small-group tutoring. No matter what, they cannot be allowed to fail. The trick to ensuring proficiency for all is to view each student as an independent learner whose timeline for mastering the material is unique to them, and to view the school year as an evolving and ongoing teach-check-and-re-teach process that is not as linear as it appears on a calendar.

Spiraled Review / Strategies to Consider:

- Daily, Weekly, Monthly Preview
- Daily, Weekly, Monthly Review
- Retesting / Parallel Assessment
- Deliberate Practice
- Spaced Practice / Distributed Practice
- Information Stations / Answer Stations
- Unit Reflection / Total Recall

Let's Stir the Soup / Strategies Not Included

As we consider the five learning levers presented in this chapter, it is fair to wonder what happened to the other methods and routines that were not included and tossed aside. What about relationships? Why not technology or gamification? How about project-based learning? Or inquiry? The truth is that any strategy or activity that helps students enjoy learning can be a tool for achievement in the hands of a great teacher. Still, the things we do to make learning enjoyable are fleeting in the absence of deep learning. The first goal of a quality education is mastering grade-level content, and the premise of this chapter is that schools should focus first on the things that move achievement the best.

While classroom activities that involve team challenges, tech integration, and hands-on projects can be used as powerful engagement tools, they are not likely to advance student achievement in the absence of the levers presented in this chapter. Though student competitions and experiments promote inquiry and problem solving, they do not directly lead to content acquisition if we do not couple them with things like discussion, writing, and error analysis. The engagement levers presented in the upcoming chapters will provide further context and examples in support of experiential learning but should not diminish the importance of explicit instruction as the first thing we must get right. In service to our industry, let us keep the discussion alive about which practices are best because the work is ever evolving. In service to children, let us involve ourselves in a never-ending search for a thrilling and meaningful school experience that is best for all kids.

3 Uncovering Personal Clarity

Academic intelligence offers virtually no preparation for the turmoil—or opportunity—life's vicissitudes bring.

—Daniel Goleman, Author and Behavioral Scientist

The muddy bog of ironies in education is so thick that we sometimes find it difficult to see our way out. So much of what we call "school improvement strategies," "classroom routines," and even "instructional best practices" are simply long-standing traditions that are presented as truths. We require students to attend school for a certain number of hours a day, and for a certain number of days a year. We pick the subjects that we deem most appropriate for all children to learn. We decide the standards. We design the lessons. We assign the grades. All the while, students are asked to trust and follow along. Even as we preach about relevancy and student voice, students typically navigate a school day not composed by them but imposed on them.

While all children are brought into the world as curious learners and creative problem-solvers, our formal system of schooling is designed around standardized lessons and assessments, as well as a taxing reliance upon teachers to present information and for students to absorb it. While explicit instruction done well provides lesson clarity and coherence, our best teachers have shown us how effective lesson design can go even further in transferring the learning and agency over to kids. As such, teacher-led instruction is not the inverse of student-centered learning. As with all best practices, the measure of effectiveness is determined by weighing who and how many are doing the thinking and who and how many are learning.

In fact, the slow rate of change across our industry to student-centered learning is a troubling sign that we need to do more. Though we have made progress, it has been plodding. In survey after survey, too many students tell us that school is uninteresting and irrelevant (Furlong et al., 1–21). They are respectfully asking for something different. In fact, if we don't deliver, their respectful persistence may turn into a full-on protest. If we were honest, we would admit that school has never been designed to be exciting, nor with student individualism in mind. School is about mass production, and it always has been. The idea of turning that reality on its head is the genesis of this chapter, beginning with lessons that imbue things like personal clarity and self-worth.

The shift is not as seismic as it sounds, and students are more than ready. Any suggestion that students cannot handle a dramatic shift in how we do schooling has more to do with adult fears than the other way around. While teachers may feel confined and restrained by standards and pacing guides, we don't want students to feel that way. What we teach might be decided by others, but the way we teach those things is up to us. Remember, the standards are not the curricula, and the curricula are not the lesson plans. In the hands of our best teachers, standards are not anchors dug deep into the muck but are more like buoys with those little lights on top that we use to navigate the lessons we design.

Lessons from the Swamp

A critical shift in how we teach grade-level content to make it at least somewhat engaging and relevant to students begins with doubling down on their inherent curiosity. Students have never lacked curiosity and wonder. They are fascinated to try new things, even if they appear tuned out in our classrooms. They dream about and ponder lots of things, sometimes in the middle of our math lessons. Just think about the endless hours that young people spend memorizing their favorite songs and mastering their favorite video games. Just consider the countless hours they spend searching for information online and learning about everything from science to politics to religion. It is a basic human condition to search out new things. We are limitless in our urge to know more.

It is not an overstatement to say that Google's success as a company has less to do with its search engine technology and more to do with our insatiable quest to know things. The company is not so much a tech giant as it is as an educational one. In fact, tapping into and capitalizing on human curiosity is a top-notch business model, and schools have a captured audience that is ready and willing to buy in. Any school or school system that designs a model built from the students' interests outward will win the marketplace.

A dramatic about-face is required if we are going to meet our students' needs and not our own. Just imagine what schooling would look like if the adults were working in service to the students, not the other way around. If we pursued that construct honestly, we would build lessons that tapped into our students' curiosity and shaped more engaged citizens. As educators, that kind of mindset shift is not so easy. Teachers are teachers for a reason. We know more than the students, so it is easy to think about schooling as a place where they come to learn from us. That is the beginning and the end, nothing more. If we do not shift this line of thinking, students will remain in an inferior position, with little to offer.

Today, in almost every school and school district, adults do all the deciding. The adults pick the assignments and assessments, select the questions to ask, and determine the right answers. The students are asked to pay close attention and take it all in, like Luke listening to Yoda in the swamp. We just keep talking and they keep listening. Come to think of it, Luke didn't really grasp much of what Yoda was saying until the young student put on a blindfold and started doing it himself.

To be clear, we can build highly engaging lessons that are also highly rigorous. We can remain committed to explicit instruction and still provide time for exploration. Researcher and scholar Daniel Muijs makes this point about balancing our approaches: "An emphasis on direct instruction and Rosenshine's principles should also not blind us to other effective strategies and processes. There is a rich research base on developing pupils' metacognition, for example, which is both rigorous and broad in scope" (Muijs 2021). Classroom instruction in the coming generations must be both explicit and applied. We can advance student mastery of core content and deepen their understanding of themselves at the same time.

The work will require teachers to find a good balance between teaching core knowledge and skills and releasing students to wonder, debate, design, and build. Make no mistake: Knowledge is not the only outcome we seek in school. It is our first mission, but not the only one. Personal awareness is just as important. If we focus only on those methods that build content acquisition, we will successfully impart knowledge upon the Jedi seated before us but leave them unsure about how all this knowledge brings purpose to their lives and how it will one day help them win the battles they will face in life against Vader and his buddies.

Table 3.1 Teacher Dilemma: Teaching Subjects Versus Students

Inside the Classroom: A Closer Look
• In a high school social studies classroom, Mr. Newsome is one of the most appreciated and celebrated teachers at his school. He is a subject area expert, and his confidence as a veteran teacher allows him to try out some cutting-edge techniques that keep his students engaged and excited. When school administrators visit his classroom, they admire his intellect and command of pacing and processes. He receives very little feedback on how to improve, and he is generally left alone to do his work. No one notices that he calls on some students more than others, mostly because the students who know the most are quick to raise their hands. Several students who speak limited English are seated together and rarely engage with Mr. Newsome or other students. Mr. Newsome is always kind and respectful, but he isn't aware that some students don't contribute very much in his class.
Considerations and Solutions • Mr. Newsome gets positive reviews and evaluations, and even the students who don't say much in class see him as a good teacher. What the teacher doesn't notice is that the students who don't contribute much do not want him to change anything. Many say that they like it this way. They are happy to do their assignments and accept their grades. The problem, of course, is that some students are learning more than others. Mr. Newsome is unaware of how much information he is sharing that is not being absorbed by some in the classroom. It is fair to say that some students are not learning the content as much as they are navigating the lessons. • **Several solutions are available** to Mr. Newsome in moving his instruction from good and somewhat interesting to highly engaging and impactful. One such move is to make small tweaks to his lesson design by (i) connecting each student to the content in some way, even if he simply asks them to find a personal connection via a reflection activity; (ii) connecting the content to the students by better understanding their interests and building those into the reading materials and activities he uses in class; (iii) ensuring that all students feel valued and engaged by building in powerful routines that check for student understanding. • **Another consideration** for Mr. Newsome is increasing his awareness of those who speak the most in class, and those who do not say much at all. He can do this by utilizing any good strategy for randomizing who he calls on. If he does this well, the teacher can determine more accurately who is learning (or not) and can strengthen his relationships with students by affirming their responses with specific praise and maybe even a personal compliment. *"Wow, what a great insight from Toby. He clearly understands how economic conditions can affect political outcomes. By the way, good luck Toby in your game tonight. We're all cheering for you."* Both the teacher and students benefit when they agree as a community that there is more to learn in school than academic content.

Making Learning Matter

To advance our work, let us imagine what school would look like if the lessons were designed to deepen each student's awareness of themselves. What do they want to explore? What do they believe in? What are their passions? Where might those interests take them in life? This shift in lesson design can be deployed in stages to make it more manageable for teachers and students. Teachers can begin by simply connecting their lessons to student hobbies like music and video games before moving into something more profound and personal to the learners. A simple shift in tone is also a good start, and that might sound something like this: *"Students, I hope our work in this unit will deepen your knowledge about the topics we are studying, but also help you find out a little bit more about yourself."*

As with all big ideas, it is best to start small. No one who has ever worked in a school would suggest that we let students run the place. We are not talking about schools without boundaries, though there are some experimental models that have attempted that. Keep in mind that the key tenet of the previous chapter is that we must build academically confident kids at all costs, beginning with mastery of reading, writing, and arithmetic. We cannot abandon that because a student wants to study something else. Academic proficiency will always be defined by expertise in core knowledge and skills. What we require our students to study in school will continue to be debated, but we cannot provide them with easier assignments in an effort to be more interesting. A wide exposure to great art and literature, as well as a deep understanding of discovery and history, cannot be compromised. We cannot stray from those foundations.

What is being presented via this chapter supports and deepens both content mastery and student engagement, not one or the other. In fact, it is fair to wonder if boredom and disengagement are compounding reasons why some students do not master core content in the first place and why some stop coming to school altogether. Marzano's research on student engagement provides four questions that can help in our lesson design (Marzano and Pickering 2010): (i) *How do I feel?* (ii) *Am I interested?* (iii) *Is this important?* (iv) *Can I do this?*

> The first two questions focus on the attention of the student, while the last two questions gauge the engagement of the students' interest in the topic. The attention questions deal with whether information from the outside world gets

> into working memory. If the information presented is not considered interesting, the working memory will not process it. Engagement is defined by importance; if the information is not deemed important, the working memory will not maintain it for long. If students do not believe they can perform the tasks, the brain will eventually reject it. (Marzano and Pickering 2010, 19)

If deep and meaningful engagement is our goal, the most profound change we can make is to embrace lessons that are not just fascinating to students but essential to their personal and social development. Let that sink in for a minute and consider what it means for our work in how we present information to students. In his book *How We Learn*, cognitive psychologist Stanislas Dehaene explores the brain's capacity to engage in new content, and to remember it. He outlines four pillars that teachers should consider for improving learning outcomes: Attention, Active Engagement, Error Feedback, and Consolidation. *Attention* highlights the brain's search for relevancy in what we are reading, hearing, and observing; *active engagement* requires learners to think and do things in response to our natural curiosities; *error feedback* demands that we correct things that don't seem right and replace them with new hypotheses that make more sense; and *consolidation* emphasizes the importance of shifting learning to long-term memory through things like repetition (Dehaene 2020).

While fun and interesting lessons will keep a student's attention, life lessons are much more compelling because they activate cognition and impact a child's social standing. More than that, the lessons we deliver can influence a student's perception of themselves and their futures. Let's be exceedingly clear on this point: There are lessons we learn in school and at home that are literally life altering, whether they are formed from traumatic events or from simple trial and error. We are forever defined by those experiences.

It should come as no surprise that a child's search for identity and purpose begins early in life and is shaped by their experiences in school. Having a good day or bad day at school can dramatically affect the way students view themselves. Each of those experiences adds up over time and shapes who we become. Across the many years from childhood to adulthood, human beings seek to understand why they exist. That journey is both spiritual (my personal beliefs) and practical (my unique skills). As such, schools play a critical role in that development whether we like it or not because what's at stake for our students is deeply personal and long-lasting.

The realities of what school has become stand in contrast to what students are seeking. The process of schooling (assignments, grades, and graduation) has always had greater emphasis than the purpose of schooling (skill-building, self-exploration, and self-worth). Every teacher will tell you that students are much more focused on fitting in than they are on things like grades and test scores. Nothing is more important to young people than how they perceive themselves. This is universally true across all schools and children. Whether a student views themselves proudly or poorly, those feelings are rooted in their home and school experiences. This provides both a challenge and opportunity for educators because the idea of impacting student lives and futures is why we became teachers in the first place. If we embrace that notion, we can design activities that build knowledge and self-esteem along a student's pathway of personal discovery.

In support of that mission, the following classroom levers are provided to help teachers create dynamic classroom experiences that help students uncover their self-worth, passions, and purpose. It is important to note that these competencies are best acquired when they are baked into the subject matter we already teach, not as a supplemental curriculum or elective course. The levers are supported by the extant research from behavioral and cognitive sciences, and from the observed classroom practices that our teachers use to make learning meaningful for kids. The following levers are critical tenets of an effective classroom, though they are not presented as strategies. Each of them can be viewed as independent of the other, as well as interdependent, so teachers can incorporate them as needed in meeting the unique needs of their schools and communities.

Cultural Awareness

Human beings are not defined by what they know, but by who they are. There are too many subtleties in play to accurately describe someone by any one characteristic, such as a job title, a college degree, or a zip code. Adults and children are too complex for that. That is why it is so important for educators to understand, appreciate, and encourage all layers of child development as part of their lesson design and delivery. Simply put, we have an obligation to help students value themselves and others. This is not only a nice thing to do, but also a critical step in developing their self-confidence and personal clarity.

We can view this as yet another yin and yang aspect of education, and as something that we have upside down in many classrooms. Though it is common for teachers to encourage mutual respect and kindness among classmates, it is difficult for students to exhibit these behaviors if they do not respect themselves first. It may come as a surprise to learn that developing a sense of pride in oneself is a prerequisite for appreciation of others. In fact, a critical step in child development begins when we get students to express their own self-confidence with full sincerity. *"I like me." "I believe in myself." "I am proud of who I am."* This goes much further than asking students to recite a set of belief statements. It is a planned and gradual process of helping students appreciate themselves. It is affirmation that has been deeply actualized over time. It is learned hopefulness. In simple terms, it is personal pride.

When human beings develop a positive self-esteem, they are more likely to stay engaged, try new things, and celebrate the accomplishments of others (Robins et al., 463–82). This sense of pride in ourselves is oftentimes cultivated at home, typically from extended families who share common bonds and traditions specific to their cultures. A child's sense of self develops around meals and family activities, and it is formalized at celebrations like birthdays and holidays. Children learn quickly where they are from, who they live with, and what they are supposed to care about. Each of us belongs to a complex culture that is informed by our upbringing and influenced by things like nationality and religion. One's culture is much more complicated than checking a box on a registration form. It is not just ethnicity or race. It is not just someone's neighborhood or lineage. Think of culture as any group of people who share common beliefs and values.

There is no doubt that many students are proud of themselves, their families, and their cultures. In fact, this is a must-have if we expect students to grow up confidently. The challenge for schools is what to do about those students who are not so proud of themselves. For some students, they are unappreciative of their culture or ashamed of their upbringing, even to the point of wishing they were someone else. Being young is challenging, but it is even harder when a child doesn't like who they are. It is difficult to expect these students to show kindness and respect to others, and it is highly unlikely they will take part honestly in the character education or cultural awareness activities we have planned.

If educators are going to develop a sense of belonging among children, incorporating simple cultural discussions around things like food, family, and holidays are great places to start. Exposing students to a wide variety of reading selections about cultures from around the world are also easy ways to foster an appreciation of others. Students will begin to see themselves in the lessons we design, and view others as not so different from themselves. This is a core value of any quality education, and it is central to being a good citizen. As with the other classroom levers, building cultural awareness must be taught and modeled for students.

For teachers who are newer to this work, a key piece of advice is to design cultural awareness activities as opportunities for students to learn about themselves first. This is where we sometimes have it backwards. Though we are quick to tell students how important it is to learn about other cultures, we do not realize that our students may be more interested in learning about their own heritage and history. It is true that we are self-consumed more than we want to admit, and we do not have to apologize for that. It is hard for most people to see beyond their own struggles. Both adults and children are overwhelmed managing their own lives, and we don't have much energy for anyone else's.

Developing a sense of classroom community is key to increasing engagement and learning, and that begins by creating an honest and secure sense of belonging for each student individually. If we get that right, then building a positive classroom culture will come easier. Some initial steps for teachers in any classroom including the following: (i) Calling on all students to contribute, and not just some students (honoring their voice); (ii) Referring to students by name and pronouncing their names correctly (honoring their culture); (iii) Affirming and praising each student for their responses (honoring their perspectives).

Student agency begins with affirmation. Self-awareness and self-efficacy are cultivated in classrooms where students are provided with enough time and space to explore what they bring to the lesson, and when their responses are heard and valued. The research and critical commentary on culturally relevant pedagogy has offered up some powerful practices for teachers, along with a few cautions that we cannot lose sight of. Renowned teacher and theorist Gloria Ladson-Billings provides fascinating insights from her years of research on how to encourage contributions from all students no matter their race, culture, or socioeconomic background.

One of her most profound reflections arrived when she learned that some educators misinterpreted her approaches by thinking that the intent was to learn *about* the students in their classrooms and not *from* the students and the unique perspectives they bring. These insights emphasize the need for lessons where students see themselves in positive situations, and by which their life experiences are valued. "By that, I mean the ability of students to draw on their own backgrounds, languages, histories, customs, and experiences ... We often use those home customs and traditions as analogies or metaphors for understanding this new culture" (Ladson-Billings 2022).

In this way, it might be helpful to think of cultural awareness as an appreciation for both the individuality and commonality among all people. Most of us are drawn to the notion that we somehow contribute to a world that is larger than ourselves, to a shared humanity. Yes, it is important for students to learn that we are more alike than different. Introducing students to other cultures is a healthy exercise in building awareness, though expecting students to relate to the plight of others and do something about it may be more than some students are ready for. Students are naturally skeptical and that is not a bad thing. Preaching to them about what they should believe or how they should act often falls on deaf ears. As with many things that adults decide on behalf of students, the kids see through it. Teachers can get frustrated quickly if they expect students to care about the things we care about, whether that's a school subject (*"I don't know why you all don't love math as much as I do."*) or a social issue (*"We should all consider adopting a pet because animal rights is an important issue."*).

Success comes best when the focus is on the students and their interests, not our own. The goal of any lesson about any topic must end with how this new knowledge makes the student, as a young person, more prepared for their life because that is what they care about. The courageous work put forth by the Collaborative for Academic, Social, and Emotional Learning (CASEL) provides teachers with tools and training aligned to this work. CASEL's mission is commendable in attempting to bring forward skills and competencies that some have questioned because they are not as discrete as learning how to add and subtract, and because some contend that school should focus on academic subjects and nothing more. This is a fair point, though it is hard to envision schools as places of deep and meaningful learning and not include activities that promote things like understanding ourselves, connecting with others, achieving our goals, and supporting our communities (see CASEL framework).

- **Classroom Example:**
  - **My Name Matters.** Let us not forget that a student's name is their most personal and precious trait. It may seem obvious for teachers

to learn their students' names, but it is less common than one might think. This is made more complicated when a student has a name that is hard for some to pronounce. There is nothing more fundamental in creating a positive classroom culture than learning all student names immediately and precisely. A teacher who fosters an environment of cultural awareness and personal clarity takes an important step in helping students reach grade-level expectations. This includes gently redirecting fellow students when they don't pronounce a classmate's name correctly.

Here's the thing. When a teacher or classmate is uncomfortable saying a student's name they will almost certainly call on or refer to that student less often. A student who is not called on to respond to a question will learn over time that their opinions are less valued. Even more troubling are the learning implications. Students who are called on less often are held less accountable for their learning. Observations of our best teachers have provided us with many strategies and processes for ensuring that all students are held accountable. Pre-planned and impromptu checks for understanding are critical tools that promote equitable outcomes. The key here is to ensure that all students are provided with opportunities to respond, that their responses are valued, and that their learning is corrected on the spot. In this way, cultural awareness is not simply a professional habit that says, "I see you, and I value you" but an instructional practice that says, "I respect you, and I will make sure that you succeed."

Cultural Awareness / Strategies to Consider:

- Civil Discourse
- Student Celebrations
- Read Aloud / Oral Storytelling
- Media / Music / Movement
- Call-and-Response / Know My Name
- Student Choice
- Family Involvement

Emotional Wellness

It should come as no surprise to hear that students cannot learn if they are unwell, physically or emotionally. While it is common for a skilled teacher to navigate a student in crisis in helping them learn the course material, crisis management is not the same thing as ongoing wellness support that helps students manage their daily struggles. It is compelling to consider how schools might pre-plan lessons that help students navigate their lives in ways that lead to improved wellness. It might be best to think of these lessons as intentionally designed to embed student coping and navigation skills. It is important to note that pulling out health and wellness competencies as separate units of study will have less impact than those that are integrated into the other subject areas. Embedded scenarios and tasks provide safe spaces for students to have hard conversations, and they are carried out in ways that model healthy and supportive classroom cultures. If done well, the lessons help students make connections to course content and deepen their sense of self at the same time.

Most teachers know that they are not teaching only their subject matter. They may prefer to, but what is listed in the job title does not always match the tasks listed in the job description. Teachers are hired to teach the students assigned to them, and those children bring emotional struggles to school each day. This is one of the most trying and heart-wrenching aspects of the job and remains a major contributor to teacher burnout. Our best teachers have navigated this role better than most because they understand that meeting students where they are is a key step in learning course content. If we follow this thread to the end, school becomes a place where students learn to manage both their academic and emotional struggles and to struggle less. Yes, we can design schools and classrooms that make the unwell well again.

It is true that the most traumatic struggles and daunting mental health needs that students face are beyond the scope of teachers. Still, many of the common pressures that come with being young can be tended to as part of our school experiences, even to the point of improving student well-being. In nearly every classroom, many of the learners seated before us are emotionally unhealthy and some are very good at hiding it. Supporting students through their formative years in navigating those struggles is well within our reach as teachers and mentors to children. While it is fair to say that teachers are hired to teach content, school has never been only about meeting a student's academic needs. In fact, some students are more in need of social-emotional skills than academic ones. Emotional wellness (e.g., believing in myself) promotes knowledge acquisition, and having content expertise (e.g., affirming my skills and intellect) promotes emotional wellness.

No one can argue the crippling effects of trauma and emotional strife on children. Knowing this, it is fair to consider whether students would be better off if schools were designed at their core to be places of positivity and affirmation. Not as a place where everybody gets a trophy, but where everybody earns a trophy. Self-efficacy by design, not by accident. It can be argued that mental well-being is harder to come by than simple intellect. Students live in a world where information is easier than ever to access, and online tools give them remote options that were previously not available.

With the advancements of artificial intelligence and computer-adapted resources, the academic coursework that we associate with school may become less necessary if the only reason school exists is for students to learn a bunch of facts and figures. This is not to suggest that AI will replace good teachers, but that certain academic skills will no longer be required because AI will do them for us. This includes basic and advanced mathematics, and most forms of writing. If that happens, we may find that students will not need teachers to help them learn but to sort out and make sense of stuff they already know.

Schools in a future sense will be uniquely positioned to teach students how to think about their learning, and how the knowledge they have gained applies to their unique life situations. This brings us back to our core mission and whether (or not) we are meeting our students' needs. While knowledge acquisition (being smart) is the primary role of schooling, that doesn't make it more important in life than emotional well-being (being contented). There is no doubt that human beings who are emotionally unwell and ill-equipped to handle it will have little chance of being successful in life. In fact, emotional clarity is so important to life success that countless studies have correlated perceived happiness to emotional intelligence, including a strong command of tangible, teachable life skills like self-control and empathy (Goleman 1995).

We should acknowledge here the long-standing contributions of behavioral scientists who study these things, including the groundbreaking work of Daniel Goleman. His now-famous books on emotionality and social intelligence have stirred a worldwide conversation for decades about the yin and yang of academic and emotional skills. Goleman and many others have cogently presented their case that adults who are intellectually brilliant but socio-emotionally deficient are rarely able to navigate successful lives by any definition. "Academic intelligence has little to do with emotional life. The brightest among us can founder on the shoals of unbridled passions and unruly impulses; people with high IQ can be stunningly poor pilots of their private lives" (Goleman 1995, 29). Of course, nobody has to tell teachers that.

If you want to test this theory, try asking teachers about their kids. They can quickly name a student who is academically smart and emotionally a wreck. Research studies have confirmed and life experience has taught us that these students will struggle once they leave behind the protections of home and school. The good news for schools is that we have seen progress in these areas, including teacher training and supplemental resources on emotional wellness. Wellness activities for students have arrived under headings like social-emotional learning (e.g., see CASEL) and trauma-informed instruction (e.g., see the Neurosequential Network). The challenge for teachers, of course, is navigating the demands of academic content standards while tending to the social-emotional needs of the students seated before us.

It might be useful to know that focusing on emotionality is not new thinking. Ancient scholars and theologians viewed emotional wellness as a virtue to be studied and taught, and they emphasized the need for society to ensure healthy temperaments among young people even before we had formal structures for schooling. To be clear, we can model and practice things like temperance and empathy in school, and we can do this within the core subject areas. If we view the teaching of social-emotional skills as adjunct to course standards, we are likely to see less success because teachers have plenty to do already. Our long history has shown us that schools already cover too much ground, from physics to physical education.

The solutions we seek will arrive by aligning and combining what we teach, not by adding more subjects. Yes, this will require cross-training of teachers and the use of interdisciplinary activities that build student self-awareness and sense of purpose. An honest conversation about student needs will help us clarify outcomes instead of adding more classes. As an example, if we agree that technology skills are critical outcomes for students, that doesn't mean we have to create a new class and make everybody take it. Wherever we land, we must elevate the importance of things like self-worth and self-care. Why? Because knowing thyself is more important than knowing thy answers.

- **Classroom Example:**
  - **Youth and Anxiety.** Students cannot be expected to do something that we have not taught them to do, even something as simple as

tying their shoes or putting their names on their papers. We show them the way (modeling), let them try it (practice), correct their mistakes (feedback), and then circle back around again (spiraled review). Yes, the process for learning how to tie your shoe is the same as it is for learning calculus. Learning things like coping mechanisms are not much different. Everything we know as adults about managing stress, from breathing techniques to meditation and exercise, is something we have learned. We were not born knowing how to cope with anxiety. We learn from experience and practice.

Teaching simple steps for students to reflect on their current circumstances and then modeling some easy coping techniques goes a long way in helping kids. This is akin to the other life skills we cover in school like study habits and conflict resolution. In providing an example, let's say a math teacher spends instructional time asking students to reflect on their right and wrong answers (error analysis). This is a best practice that affirms a student's ability to reflect, refocus, and do better next time. In fact, it exemplifies schooling. It presents the learning process in the simplest of terms, getting better at something through direct instruction and explicit reflection. If that is so, then it is not a reach to ask students to reflect on how they are coping with mild to moderate anxieties in their lives.

Students might be struggling with friends or family (usually both). Maybe they didn't make the honor roll or the cheerleading squad, or maybe there has been endless arguing and door-slamming at home. No matter what it is, teachers can use reflection activities that are not much different than asking them how they processed a problem on a test and what they might do differently next time. Students can share their responses (or not) privately with other students, and the teacher can select one or two powerful responses (or not) and use them anonymously as examples of how students are developing coping skills. Interdisciplinary approaches can also be effective and relatable for students. No matter the subject area, teachers can raise up the famous people we study in school as examples (e.g., a well-known athlete, an important historical figure, or a character in a book) to highlight how they struggled, sequenced, and defeated whatever demons they faced.

Emotional Wellness / Strategies to Consider:

- Morning Meetings
- Community Circles
- Positive Framing
- Authentic Praise / No Sarcasm
- Routines and Processes

Content Relevance

Let's face it. We can teach students fractions, functions, and forces with little or no sense of how this relates to their lives and communities. Though core knowledge is central to what we do in school, it comes with skepticism from our students. Most students will go through the motions with us, but they will tune us out if they are not buying what we are selling. In a twist of irony, relevancy has always mattered more to the learner than it has to the teacher. In fact, it is not uncommon to find educators and commentators belittling the idea of relevant curricula, as if giving into student demands for more engaging stuff to read and do is surrendering our intellectual high ground. We know that teachers are enchanted by their subject areas, and they will defend a specific novel or invention or historical period as if someone just made fun of their best friend. Language arts teachers love words and books, and science teachers love exploration and discovery. We are content nerds. Our passions about content are deep-seated and personal, not just professional. It is as if we are asking students to join us in our passions, and some do. In our excitement, we invite students in but sometimes miss opportunities to bring them along.

In the end, engagement is not simply about making something interesting. It is about making learning personal and approachable, not simpler or easier. *I can relate to this subject or topic. It is relevant to me.* This does not mean that everything we teach in school must be practical. Abstract concepts and classical studies can be fascinating to kids, but learning these things will not last if students don't connect to them in some way. Think of relevancy as learning that is contextualized. It should illuminate my understanding of myself and the world around me.

We know that adult learners and children process new information quickly and determine if they care about learning this stuff in the first place. They do this in part by visualizing how it situates into their lives (Dehaene 2020). To the learner, knowledge without context is simply trivia. *I find this interesting, but it's not really that important. Therefore, I reject it and will not retain it.* On the other hand, knowledge with context brings wisdom. *I find this fascinating, and it might help me manage my life better and see things that I might have missed before.*

Relevancy is a key lever in helping students become not just smart but savvy. Students can utilize the knowledge and skills they learn in school more effectively if we help them sort out the puzzle pieces and uncover the cool picture that emerges. Nothing is learned in isolation. It all matters, from the collapse of the Roman Empire to the fall of the Berlin Wall. As teachers, we are tasked with helping students to see why knowledge matters. It is not just to win trivia contests.

One of the barriers we face is viewing the learning tasks we present to students as literal and the steps to mastering them as sequential, as if learning a discrete skill or standard builds on the next one in perfect order. Though learning sometimes goes like that, it oftentimes does not. While a properly designed scope and sequence is a great tool in keeping us focused, teaching is not learning. Only learning is learning. In real classrooms with real kids, it is not uncommon for a student to master one skill and then whiff on the next one, only to come back around later and figure it all out. In real classrooms with real kids, learning is more like Jenga than dominos. The end game is getting students to see how the skills and concepts they are learning connect in ways that help them now and in the future, and then pray that we get to that point before the whole thing comes tumbling down.

As hard as it is for students to understand, the value of any great education is not to learn things but to be learned. Yes, we should continue to expose children to the best that has ever been thought and known (we see you, Matthew Arnold). Students need wide exposure to great works and thinkers. Relevancy then is the degree to which students connect these things to what they already know. As such, relevancy is measured not by how much they are going to use what they are learning but how much they care about it. Teachers cannot determine that, only students can. If we get it right, students will enjoy learning and want more of it. In the end, learning to do math is not the same thing as valuing math, and learning to write is not the same thing as being a writer. Sadly, we have many students who read well, but who don't like to read. There are too many students in too many schools who can recite the elements in the periodic table but who find science and nature uninteresting and irrelevant.

This brings us to a dilemma that cuts to the core of what we believe. Does our interest in designing fun and interesting learning activities increase student engagement but impede content acquisition? Our teachers have answered this for us. Yes, there are many examples of engaging class activities that students enjoy but do not advance learning. Still, the opposite is also true. As always, the teacher's effectiveness in designing and delivering the lesson determines the outcome. In our most successful classrooms, student engagement is not synonymous with excitement. It is more cerebral than that; it has cognitive purpose. Just because students are having fun building something or blowing it up does not mean they are learning. Our best teachers build engaging lessons to advance student mastery of core content, not as a substitute for it.

A key step for teachers who want to build relevant lessons is planning ahead so they can ask relevant questions and include authentic examples. This invites students into the conversation and helps them view the lesson at hand as something more than an academic exercise. We all have seen students engrossed in a great novel and eager to retell a basic understanding of the characters, plot, and theme. The students know the novel and its content but nothing more. This is sometimes referred to as "teaching the novel." It is no different than teaching the math or the science or the arts. In the end, students are exposed to new material but will not remember much. Students are simply following along, and content knowledge is fleeting. The students are not smarter, and they are no wiser.

It is fair to wonder about the purpose of schooling if it is not to create informed and involved citizens. There is little reason to learn how to read and write if we don't plan to say anything, or tell a story, or pitch an idea. This may be hard to hear but some students truly believe that the subjects they are studying in school are only required for the purpose of obtaining a degree. The most troubling example is when students tell us that they view reading as a skill they need only to pass the state assessments. We have reached a disturbing place in our industry if students view reading as an irrelevant skill. If we get nothing else right, we can regain our influence and standing as leaders in learning by creating experiences by which students are not just functionally literate, but they enjoy reading. We owe students at least that much.

We know that school as a social construct was designed to develop good workers and reliable citizens, though some poke fun at that notion and view things like being a good neighbor and volunteering in the community as not worthy of our time in school. A new generation of young people may not see it that way, not because they want to be more neighborly but because they want to learn things that will help them help themselves. Gen Alpha and Beta are not hesitant to voice their demands, and they will be quick to call out old bureaucracies in favor of something that is more personal to them. Relevancy on those terms might lead to curriculum that is issue-centered, not subject-centered, and assignments that are hands-on and hyper-local. Some of these suggestions may be viewed as counterculture, but they are not counterintuitive. Don't forget that we have a system of schools forged out of traditions. They are easy and familiar to us, so we just keep doing them.

- **Classroom Example:**
  - **Life Riddles and Relevancy.** A simple entry point for teachers who want to make their lessons more relevant is connecting them to local community issues that students can relate to. The entire lesson could be designed around a real or fictional case study, or a teacher can simply begin the unit with a relevant question or challenge to spark student imagination. As an example, a math teacher could begin a new unit with the following challenge: *"Students, let's say you are cooking dinner for your family by following a very precise recipe. At the last minute, two other families call and invite themselves over. Your mom is freaking out but agrees to invite them. Your family has four people. The hungry neighbors will arrive with seven additional people to feed. In our upcoming unit, we are going to work with proportions to help solve these kinds of challenges."*

    As another example, a social studies class might start with the following case study: *"Students, let's picture a scenario where you and your teenage friend are driving and get pulled over for blasting your music too loud. The officer cites you for disturbing the peace, and the fine is $275. You believe that your rights as a citizen should allow you to play music in your car as loud as you want because the only people harmed by loud music are the ones in the car. In our next unit, we are going to study our systems of government to better understand where our rights begin and end, and what you can do to fight back against laws and policies that you don't think are fair and just."* These are simple examples, but there are countless other lesson "hooks" that teachers can create related to any subject and grade level. Additionally, any curriculum unit for any subject can be built around problems of local importance (e.g., water quality, beach erosion, immigration, farming, transportation, utility costs, housing costs, etc.).

Teachers can enhance these lessons further by including a brief role-play where students are asked to apply their skills. Skilled teachers routinely use case studies and role-play to encourage student discourse and synthesis of key concepts. Think of these types of activities as four-dimensional advanced organizers that require students to think, develop, apply, and redeploy their learning. Even if teachers are not comfortable with things like riddles and role-play, every lesson can be adapted slightly to provide students with some agency in their learning. Students can be given choices regarding the poems, novels, and articles they read, as well as options for the research topics and experiments they are assigned to. Ponder for a moment how strange it must feel to students to have little or no say in the subjects they take or the things they read. Yes, it is ironic that we ask students what their favorite subjects are, knowing that we were the ones who picked the subjects for them. Any connections that teachers make to student lives and families will also resonate with students. If we get these steps right, students will see school as something that happens with them, not to them, and they will view the skills they are learning as tools for tackling personal struggles or civic dilemmas they may soon face.

Content Relevance / Strategies to Consider:

- Flexible Assignments / Choice
- Virtual Field Trips
- Puzzles / Word Problems
- Cross-Disciplinary / Hexagonal Thinking
- Family / Community Connections
- Role-Play

The Psychology of Hope

The emerging research in organizational behavior science provides school districts with some intriguing insights. The lessons gleaned from Positive Organizational Scholarship (POS) are especially notable in making the case for deeper, richer workplace experiences as a way of impacting measurable outcomes. Think of this new psychology as the science of positivity. Studies regarding the ecology of human relationships within the workforce point to the following four qualities of successful employees: self-efficacy, hope, optimism, and resiliency. This topic will be covered in more depth in Chapter 5. Still, there is much to consider here as we design lessons that meet our students' current needs and prepare them for adulthood.

Though this may be difficult to consider, it is fair to wonder whether the systems we have in place across schools and districts are designed to tamp down such things as self-efficacy and resiliency or relegate them to second-tier status. There is certainly a thin thread that connects top-down structures to discrete outcomes that can be monitored and measured. As such, any suggestion that outcomes like kindness and respect will be valued over algebra and geometry is a hard sell, not so much because the system doesn't value kindness but because it doesn't trust what it cannot quantify. This is a practical reality that we must overcome if we are going to lift up workplace skills or life skills as legitimate outcomes. As with any topic or skill we learn in school, there are critical questions that we must be ready to answer: What is being taught? How is it best taught? How is it best assessed? How is it reinforced? Why does it matter?

There is much more to consider in seeking dramatic systems changes. To this end, the ideas presented in this chapter will not rid us of our struggles. Still, they are part of a set of workable solutions designed to make learning more engaging and relevant for children. In the end, going to school should be fascinating for kids, and that demands learning experiences that are transcendent, even sublime. School as a place where students are less likely to tell us, "Man, I am bored," and more likely to shout out, "Wow, I discovered something new today. I found out something about myself, about what I stand for, and I plan to do something about it."

4 Finding Creative Purpose

If you run an education system based on standardization and conformity that suppresses individuality, imagination, and creativity, don't be surprised if that's what it does.

—Ken Robinson, Ph.D., Author and Educator

In the end, we all seek the same things. We seek family and friendships. We seek health and happiness. We seek purpose. Students search for these things along with us. The things we seek are elusive and alluring, which makes them universally desired. To be clear on this point, we cannot have great schools if we do not help students find the things they desire. Yes, schooling is a lot like parenting. It's our job to provide for their needs, and we owe them a school experience that prepares them to pursue a life well-lived. In the end, the true validation of our success as educators is the degree that we advance students through a system that provides them with increasing skills, purpose, and hope. The goal of any successful lesson design and delivery is to journey students through a series of well-played questions and rigorous tasks that require more of them than they ever thought possible, including bouts of failure, sparks of brilliance, and mind-blowing moments of discovery that help them mature into confident, compassionate, and creative young adults.

In our schools, we must take this challenge of building great citizens both literally and figuratively. Students simply cannot leave us without knowing how to read, write, and tie their shoes. Without a doubt, they must know as well how to speak thoughtfully and discuss things respectfully. Yes, they should know their history and understand their place in it. They should have broad experience with researching and problem-solving and have a great command of the best methods for doing so. If we get our lessons right, students will find the riddles and challenges of life as something they are eager to solve, even if they cannot yet solve them. To be sure, our schools should provide students with the time and space to get their hands dirty, to fix things, and to sing and dance. More than anything else we can offer them, students must graduate from our schools as proud of themselves. *I did this. I created this. I designed something or built something or performed something that I am incredibly proud of. I am a better version of myself than I used to be. I am more than I ever thought I would be, and there is more of me to come.*

This is quite a difficult task with all the other things we are balancing. It is fair to debate what things students should learn in school vs. home as long as we agree that learning skills like counting and spelling are only important if we plan to use them. Giving students an opportunity to create things gives them a chance to use their academic skills and see value in the math, science, and literacy content they are learning in class. In his legendary book on creativity in schools, Ken Robinson explores the idea that academic subjects should be taught to help students develop approaches or perspectives for solving problems (e.g., an arts perspective or a STEM approach). "In a sense, there is really no such thing as an academic subject. There are only academic ways of looking at things" (Robinson 2015, 141). If we follow this line of thinking to the end, then our role as subject-matter experts is to ensure our students master core content and can employ those skills via tasks that require logic, reasoning, and situational awareness.

Creativity as Cognition

Creativity is humanity's divine gift. It arrives at some point while we are young and expresses itself uniquely within each of us, whether that's fixing our cars or painting our nails. Without a doubt, there is a spiritual wonder that lives within every single person. If it is true that we breathe in information, then it must be true that we breathe out inspiration. *I can build a better video game or computer app. I can design a better car or bicycle or skateboard. I can invent a new dance move. I can open a new business.* These are the things we all dream about, and they provide practical considerations for educators as we debate the purpose of schooling. Even for those of us who never get the chance to cure a disease or go to the moon, we have limitless creative ambition. There is much to be gained in school by tapping into those ambitions. Aristotle said it best: "Wonder is the source of our desire for knowledge" (Aristotle, Metaphysics 1.2.982).

Creativity is the product of talent and curiosity, not one or the other. As teachers, we can either ignore this reality or lean into it. Creative hunger is fulfilled in a thousand ways, from cooking and quilting to fishing and fashion.

Yes, we are all creatives. In our classrooms, it might be best to view creativity as productive genius. It is the highest form of cognition, a place where learning and doing are symbiotic and seamless. In a practical sense, creativity is closely aligned to enterprise, a place where understanding and applying come together. Students as problem-solvers, both entrepreneurial and industrious. Not only designing and drawing but building and marketing. In fact, it has become increasingly common for students to open their own businesses, whether that is a fledging lemonade stand or a thriving online store. We have learned that students can be trusted to do much, much more than we think. They are fully capable of conceiving a new idea and seeing it through, and school is a great place for trial and error.

The lessons we design and activities we require should give students practice in the adventures that come with creating things. It should be noted that creating anything requires a great deal of technical skill and dedicated practice. If we are applying our math, science, and literacy skills, it makes sense for students to pound a nail or boil an egg. If we could reshape the required vs. elective courses, we might shift to something that feels more connected and interdisciplinary for students, where things like the engineering design process and instructional technology are seamlessly infused into core content. This requires intentionality as to our course design and progression. We cannot allow students to spend years and years in school without substantive opportunities to master hardware and software skills, construction tools and machinery, and-or musical instruments. The positive impacts of career-technical and arts education are well-documented, and there is no sensible way forward in designing great schools without continuing that investment.

Whatever schooling becomes for future generations, it will require students to spend more time doing and less time listening. In a competitive marketplace, students and families will demand a school experience that is challenging and compelling. Our best teachers are good at this already. They have found a way to cover course standards and develop student skills through activities that are collaborative and applied. They successfully incorporate movement and discussion as essential routines for learning. Experiential activities that are tied to grade-level standards come in many forms, from planting gardens to testing water samples. Hands-on learning can begin in the earliest grades and can be infused easily into core coursework. This does not upend our commitment to direct instruction. It actually advances our best practices, because it requires both high-quality explicit instruction and applied practice. The key outcome here is creating experiences that lead to improved skill and accuracy in math, science, language arts, and social studies by providing opportunities for students to showcase their new knowledge. All activities in school should lead to better command of academic disciplines, as well as an appreciation for learning itself. Students deserve opportunities to showcase their learning, and that requires lessons that demand their expertise.

Control Versus Command

If we want to embrace learning that is truly student-centered, we must come to grips with the idea that students should be the ones bringing energy and ideas to the classroom, not just the teacher. This does not mean that teachers should relinquish the qualities that make them effective and likable, like enthusiasm, positivity, and humor. There may not be a study yet to confirm this, but if we ever get to a place where teachers stop high-fiving kids then formal education may cease to exist. Our favorite teachers are our favorites for a reason. It is hard to separate teachers from their personalities, and we should not try to because students cling to the teachers who they relate to best, and that can lead to powerful mentor relationships that are life changing. At the same time, the teacher who is most popular is not always the one who impacts learning the most. This is an important distinction when we consider what we are observing as we enter a classroom.

The ideas presented via this chapter celebrate teacher actions that release control over to students not only so they enjoy learning but because they learn more. The definition of effective instruction must always be tied to achievement outcomes, and the teacher actions that give voice and choice over to kids must be developed to encourage academic discourse and higher-order thinking with a clear intent to improve learning. For this reason, student-centered learning is highly reliant on the teacher if it is going to work. The teacher is the teacher for a reason, and it is illogical to give students free range to explore aimlessly when there is an expert in the room.

The shifts described here move us to a place where master teachers give way to student voice and choice as a way of creating master students who can do things without someone holding their hands. There are too many examples of students who follow along and get good grades but who cannot do for themselves. A troubling sign is when students are asked to practice technical skills without a clear understanding of why they need those skills or how they are leading to something more profound. Sadly, it is not uncommon to see students learning a skill like close reading or underlining by following the teacher's directions in a rote manner that is more like filling out a worksheet than learning a new approach that might deepen their appreciation of literature. More than that, teachers can get so caught up in applauding a student's excellent use of underlying techniques that everyone forgets that the goal is proficient comprehension, not proficient underlining. . .

Across education, we have made the mistake too many times of validating student responses when they recite back to us exactly what we want to hear with rote weariness. In many cases, they are just repeating our words and everyone is playing along. In his famous essay *Lilies that Fester*, C. S. Lewis makes a compelling case for some balance between what is demanded by the teacher (i.e., standards) and what is desired by the student, things like personal exploration, authentic debate, and original thought. Lewis claims that a child's path to intellectual maturity via our traditional models is defined by conformity in the way a child can calculate, recite, and rebuff in such a way as to sound like everyone else. "The boy will not get good marks unless he produces the kind of responses, and the kind of analytic method, which commend themselves to his teacher" (Lewis 1952, 43).

Of course, there is nothing wrong with this as long as you're the teacher. Still, it is fair to question whether a new generation of entrepreneurial young scholars will arise from a system where children are "trained in the art of simulating orthodox responses" (Lewis 1952, 43). If nothing else, the opportunities provided in tackling real-world problems give rise to students who dare original thoughts and solutions. In keeping our focus on extant research and teacher best practice, the levers provided in this chapter are commonly and effectively used by teachers across grade levels to open up dialogue, encourage free expression, and advance learning through upskilling and practice. Think of this as the application of language arts, science, and civics with a purpose that goes beyond underlining to reveal a world of philosophy and politics and personal ambition that students are eager to know more about.

Table 4.1 Teacher Dilemma: Learning Without Purpose

Inside the Classroom: A Closer Look
• In her ESE intervention classroom, Mrs. Langley cares deeply about her students and is a veteran high school teacher with strong classroom procedures and skills. She provides her students with critical organizational skills they need to succeed, and she reviews and reteaches some of the core content they are learning in their other classes. The students benefit from her approaches as evidenced by their improved grades and study habits. The students trust their teacher and follow her directives. Despite her success and expertise, Mrs. Langley is frustrated because several students have told her that they don't enjoy school very much and they are considering dropping out as soon as they are legally allowed. This is a troubling cycle that she has witnessed for years. What she doesn't know is that when her students talk about being bored, they are referring to her class as well.
Considerations and Solutions • Mrs. Langley believes she is doing everything she has been taught to do as a teacher, and she is probably right. She has been tasked with making sure her students keep their grades up, and she knows that study skills are what her students are lacking. While it is true that her students need better habits to succeed in school, those are not the most pressing concerns for the students themselves. Her students are worried about things unrelated to school, including their own family's financial health and violence they witness in their homes and neighborhoods. Mrs. Langley's students have not given much thought to what they are going to do after high school. They are all capable, but they are unaware of their options and see little connection between school and life. • **In finding a solution**, Mrs. Langley might serve her school's wants and the students' needs better by connecting things like reading and math to better job options after high school. As a start, the teacher might utilize applied learning to help students see the connections between the two. In any classroom, applied learning can be used to reinforce academic knowledge and skills, and to advance student executive functioning and workplace skills. The teacher might even connect her review of key academic concepts like measurement to hands-on tasks that require students to use a ruler, a wrench, or a needle and thread. An important step in making this solution effective is connecting the lesson activities to student practice and upskilling in reading and math skills. • **As another consideration**, Mrs. Langley might also connect her assignments to student voice as a way of enhancing their interest in school and providing clarity regarding their futures. Any lesson can include a brief or extended opportunity to discuss, create, and perform. A science lesson about the water cycle can lead to a great discussion about water quality and community inequities. A reading assignment about family heritage can lead to a lesson in genealogy, a trip to the local library, interviews with family members, and maybe a performance assessment like a spoken word poem or video short. As a veteran teacher who cares about her students, Mrs. Langley can take her instructional practice to another level.

Applied Learning / Civic Involvement

The elusive search for genuine student engagement is something we could solve tomorrow if we really wanted to. Students have been clamoring for more hands-on learning experiences since the advent of schooling. Despite our progress, many classrooms are focused more on textbooks and tasks than exploration and experimentation. Our progress has been ravaged by a maelstrom of unhealthy objectives and misinformed opinions, the most glaring of which is that students who are busy doing something would be better served by direct instruction from the teacher. Some of these misunderstandings are not political but practical. Many are convinced that applied learning takes too much time or that it is a culminating activity at the end of a lesson (a project, for example). In fact, applied learning is viewed by many educators as akin to project-based learning and even inquiry-based learning. Applied learning as defined here is not that.

The instructional approaches described here are much more foundational and connected to core instruction, not as supplemental or even optional. A key step in helping us understand and utilize this critical lever is viewing any let's-get-our-hands-dirty instructional approach as embedded into our classroom routines in a way that reinforces academic knowledge and skills. As with most things in education, the terms we use are less important than the outcomes we seek. If students are not smarter and wiser as a result, we should not be doing it. The truth is, designing and delivering any type of applied learning task is messy even if our students and families are asking for more of it. Learning by doing is a great practice but only if we design it right, and getting it right is more important than abandoning the idea for something easier. Claiming that performance tasks, projects, and labs are not effective because we oftentimes do them poorly is like saying that students should not contribute to classroom discussion because their answers are sometimes wrong. The challenge for us as educators is to accept what is difficult and get better at it.

If we think about learning by doing as methods for collaboration, discussion, and movement, then it may seem less daunting. In fact, school may be the only place where we are expected to learn from listening than by doing. We know in our guts that this is not best for kids. It is simply impossible to be a good mechanic or a great dancer by reading about it. The same is true for writing or math or scientific inquiry. Reading from a textbook and taking a few quizzes is simply not enough if I am not allowed to practice in a way that provides a great challenge and piques my interest. Applied or experiential learning with clearly stated objectives is part of a set of solutions to promote equitable learning outcomes and mitigate achievement gaps. These approaches also have the promise of providing relief to teachers from the trauma of scripted curricula and lessons.

The good news in implementing applied learning activities is that we have many success stories, so learning from our colleagues may be the best way forward. The infusion of science, technology, engineering, and math (STEM) activities in our classrooms has been a giant step forward for our industry, so any discussion about what works best should begin there. Our STEM colleagues have been at the forefront of innovative and engaging lesson design for decades, even with the missteps we have made along the way. Remember, messy always proceeds mastery.

Though STEM clubs and robotics teams are great enhancements to any school, the most lasting benefits will come when we view applied learning not as an elective or a club but as an approach to content instruction. This includes applied literacy and social sciences, by which students are using their reading, writing, and research skills to create or design something that impacts their lives and neighborhoods. This could be as simple as a letter to the City Council, or as ambitious as a citywide campaign to fund a local pet shelter. The benefits of applied learning include a greater sense of community and improved executive functioning skills. This is consistent with the running narrative that school is about raising up good citizens and not about passing tests.

We have come a long way in growing support among educators and policymakers for teaching executive functioning and workplace skills, sometimes called "soft skills" or "durable skills." In a competitive workforce, these skills are often in short supply and can widen an employee's job prospects and chances for advancement. Of course, many states and school districts have already embedded these expectations into their standards and course designs. As an example, the North Carolina Portrait of a Graduate continuum allows for deeper student learning and skill attainment across its K-12 spectrum. The initiative promotes a "student's ability to adapt, to collaborate, to communicate, to think critically, to show empathy, to learn, and to take personal responsibility." The state resources include student "I can" statements that align to each durable skill or concept. The following is just one example: "I can present information, findings, and supporting evidence clearly and directly, addressing alternative or opposing perspectives to allow listeners to follow my line of reasoning" (North Carolina Department of Public Instruction).

A critical step forward is figuring out how to fold these skills into our lessons in a way that advances content acquisition. As with academic skills like counting and factoring, workplace skills cannot be learned in isolation and without proper context and repeated practice. We have made the mistake too many times of adding new demands on schools without knowing exactly how and where they fit into the curriculum (e.g., character education and health education). An important caution in developing hands-on projects or labs is considering how students will increase their skills and knowledge and clarifying the pacing and purpose of the activity. Remember, we should never forsake learning in our efforts to be interesting. Unfortunately, there are many examples of students having a good time drawing or building things where not much learning is happening, and a lot of time is wasted. Poor implementation is not evidence that hands-on learning is a misguided approach. It simply means that we must be good at it for it to be effective, much like the other routines in our classrooms. As mentioned, even powerful best practices like group work and turn-and-talk can be less than effective if we do not have clear directions and objectives or if the pacing is off.

Wherever this work takes us, learning by doing must become a primary methodology if we are going to solve the "school is boring" apparition that haunts us still. Whether students are learning to write or solve or measure, they can do those things outside under the trees or on the lawn or in the school parking lot. They can practice and showcase such things in their classrooms and neighborhoods via projects that require them to research, plan, falter, and succeed. These activities can be devised as culminating tasks that assess student learning or as lesson hooks that engage students to think and explore material at the beginning of a unit. No matter the form or format, applied learning can greatly enhance student confidence and creativity, not to mention the potential to quench our thirst to figure things out and compete against each other. As with other classroom practices, cognitive engagement is key if we want these activities to be properly seated as drivers for learning.

- **Classroom Example:**
  - **Building is Better.** Students can improve their understanding of processes like scientific inquiry and practice skills like measurement

if we let them explore the world around them. This can be as simple as taking an elementary classroom outside to measure the distance between the library and the cafeteria or approximate the height of the playground slide and then confirm their predictions through testing. Building things from birdhouses to butterfly gardens also provides endless opportunities to practice math and science. The key ingredients to these activities are purpose, pacing, and assessment. While there is certainly a time and place for fun activities at school (a school carnival, for example), classroom activities should always lead to learning. Students will learn more and have more fun if the hands-on activity we have planned has purpose and structure to it. Just like adults, students tend to perform better when they understand why they are doing something. The purpose of building a birdhouse may be as simple as practicing length, width, and angles. In this example, the assessment is not a quiz but the birdhouse itself.

Remember that perfect execution of the task is the goal for each child. We cannot allow any student to make a lopsided birdhouse and then tell them how proud we are of their efforts. If a student struggles, we must help them understand how they got it wrong and help them fix it. The applied learning activities explored in this chapter are consistent with an embedded curriculum model. This provides teachers across subject areas to partner if they wish on projects that enhance STEM skills like design and measurement as well as literacy skills like writing and speaking. In observing our most impactful teachers in action, their lesson designs and outcomes are explicit and authentic. It really does not make sense to ask students to build a birdhouse and then require them to write an essay comparing different types of birds. It is more compelling to have them build something and then prepare a short talk explaining what they learned and what they plan to do with their new birdhouse.

Student presentations and performances are excellent methods for evaluation and assessment of student learning. Any type of project or performance can be utilized to assess knowledge and skill, as long as we provide students with constructive feedback when their work falls short. Teachers of core content subjects would do well to observe the feedback loops that are skillfully embedded into applied arts courses like drama and band. Explicit practice and feedback are part of the daily routines in these classrooms, and performances are adjudicated either by a single judge or a panel of experts that holds each student to the same high standard. These structures can be easily adapted to evaluate student writing, speaking, and presentation assignments.

Applied Learning / Strategies to Consider:

- Learning Outside / Field Research
- Service Learning / Volunteering
- Community Involvement / Activism
- Case Studies / Issue-Based Scenarios
- Classroom Labs and Experiments
- Hands-On Projects / Team Challenges

Student Voice

The most powerful and observable outcome of a confidence-based curriculum is student voice. If we ever reach the pinnacle of best practice in curriculum design and instructional methodology, we will arrive at a place where students develop a distinctive voice. They will have informed opinions on many things, and they will know how to frame their thoughts with great clarity and elocution. Students and teachers will view school not only as a place to learn new things but as a rich marketplace where they can have their say about the things they already know. To be honest, we are as ready as ever to build schools like these. All we have to do now is speak it into existence. Any school in any town can be designed as a boundless platform for self-expression, a vibrant space where students consider profound ideas and balance confounding solutions. In this space, students learn to wonder, predict, ponder, and refute their own ideas and those of their classmates. They learn to accept defeat, fall gracefully, and get up again.

As with all things in school, the advancement of student agency in the classroom begins and ends with the teacher. Students cannot set out to have agency if the teacher has not set the conditions for it. In short, teachers either encourage or discourage student voice. There is no in between. As a starting point, voice can be defined as welcoming student insights during a lesson, even to the point of honoring their wishes as to what they might want to read or research. Valuing the students seated before us and celebrating what they bring to the classroom is a critical point along the engagement number line, but there are many others to consider. Voice can also be defined as the explicit development of student literacy skills so they can make credible arguments. This requires students to practice and master the art of persuasion, including a strong command of presentation, performance, and other forms of creative expression.

As a cross-disciplinary approach, encouraging and developing student voice requires schools to embed skills like writing and rhetoric across grade levels and subject areas. Things like oratory and presentation skills must have clear standards for quality with ongoing feedback loops. In learning from our colleagues in the visual and performing arts, schools can encourage a community of learners who are not afraid to present something, even in draft form. The evaluation loop can be tied to student grades or not, and it ends only when a student masters their craft and celebrates their accomplishments. Here again is where exemplary models come into play. A well-designed evaluation rubric with exemplars are forms of success criteria that promote equitable outcomes in everything from a biology lab to a band performance.

Student voice in the most authentic terms is more akin to self-efficacy. *I do not only have a say in my school and my assignments, but in what I believe and who I will become. My experiences and perspectives are my strengths. I am inquisitive. I am thoughtful. I am unique.* The interdependence of the classroom levers provided throughout this text becomes clear when student voice is the ultimate outcome. Students can discover and cultivate their voices only in classrooms where robust academic discussion is spirited and cultural awareness is fostered. Across our industry, we have convincing evidence that if a teacher believes a child is brilliant, they will become so.

It is a common refrain in professional sports for a coach to say, "We are what our record says we are." If a team has lost most of its games, then it cannot claim to be any good. The team cannot explain away its unsuccess by blaming their losses on a couple of bad calls or dumb luck. The team is what its record says it is. This is true as well in our classrooms. The students are who we have allowed them to be. If students are struggling, that is on us. If they are timid and unskilled, that is on us. If we wish for them to be smart, compassionate, and articulate, we can build schools and lessons to get them there. Though we have no control over the powerful influences in their homes and neighborhoods, we directly impact their academic and social skills and outcomes. Graduating students who have a distinguishing voice and thriving self-confidence will arrive via a perfect mixture of skills and experiences, most of which are learned in school. Like confidence, voice is not given, it is earned.

- **Classroom Example:**
  - **Voice as Perspective.** In most classrooms and with most lessons, the teacher's voice is the most prominent. This has been true for as long as each of us can remember. Not only do teachers talk more than the kids do, but the teacher also affirms what is right and acceptable for every thought and insight that students offer in class. This is a common reality that is hard to hear, but also hard to dispute. It is necessary that teachers maintain order in their classrooms, while imparting their own expertise of their content and craft. Still, if we are not careful, students will acquire a great deal of knowledge and skill across many years of schooling but not form shrewd opinions of the content or sound opinions of themselves.

    A shift in school from teacher as content expert to teacher as academic coach and mentor is not far afield. Our most successful teachers acknowledged and embraced that shift long ago. Students might apply their learning by collecting water samples from nearby ponds. They might even hypothesize, measure, and test things. Still, no degree of content expertise is a match for having a healthy awareness and informed opinions about ecological systems and environmental threats, and to respectfully articulate those viewpoints. A not-so-obvious juxtaposition is found when we observe lessons in history and literature, and students are asked to identify the themes they see but not required to construct their own. Our best teachers are able to skillfully move students from recognizing correct patterns (identifying) to anticipating them (predicting). Many teachers can get students to successfully recite the literary themes in *The Great Gatsby* or identify the rhetorical devices in *A Letter from the Birmingham Jail* but cannot quite get students to replicate those threads in their own writing. Developing voice requires students to learn from what they are reading and hearing so they can adopt those techniques.

    A truly rewarding moment in any classroom comes when a student has an idea or solution that the teacher never considered before. We see this a lot in art classes when students are asked to draw or paint their own interpretations of things, even among students in the earliest grades. The same wonderment arises when we ask students to write or say something original. By this definition, student voice is not just speaking. It is perspective. Those perspectives arrive in many forms, but only when we give them space in our classrooms to root and bloom.

Student Voice / Strategies to Consider:

- Student-Led Conferences
- Student-Led Advocacy / Leadership
- Discussion and Debate
- Authentic Writing and Speaking
- Creative Expression / Performances
- Oral Presentation

A Gradual Realization of Self

Educators seeking new and better methods to engage students have embraced applied learning and related ideas to increase agency and voice. In fact, many promising trends are emerging across the globe. In 2018, Singapore made worldwide headlines when it shifted from a highly structured and competitive school system designed to rank and order children to something much more personal than that, with an ambitious plan to graduate children who are highly skilled, but also creatively minded. Similar changes have arrived in Finland, a long-standing leader in innovative practices. The country has scrapped traditional school subjects for a multidisciplinary approach that it calls "phenomenon-based" learning. In essence, Finland is taking a thematic approach by teaching content and skills though broader topics like climate change and community building.

For purposes of this text, we will describe these new curriculum frameworks as narrow and concentric at the same time, including lesson expectations that deepen foundational knowledge and skills and apply student thinking to new situations. Wherever we land, the outcomes we seek must be highly scaffolded in building student competencies for tackling whatever life brings their way. This work is not as far-fetched as it may seem, as many creative interpretations are underway right now in forward-thinking school districts and global think tanks. For schools and districts that have not adopted measurable workplace or life skills, here are five to get the discussion started:

- **Outcome:** A precise ability to write and speak effectively, to state your case persuasively, and to disagree respectfully. **Skills / Topics:** A broad and rich vocabulary; simple and complex sentence structures; rhetorical devices; power nouns and verbs.
- **Outcome:** A confident number sense to navigate and solve problems as they arise, and to promote sound financial planning and budgeting. **Skills / Topics:** Data analysis; statistics; forecasting; ratio and proportion; cost accounting; interest rates.
- **Outcome:** A deep understanding of laws and policies that impact our daily lives, and how involved citizens can influence change. **Skills / Topics:** Government structures; case law; elections and political influence; separation of powers.
- **Outcome:** A strong grasp of key historical figures, advancements, and conflicts, and why revolution and change are recurring themes across generations. **Skills / Topics**: Economic and governmental philosophies; politics and power; freedom; corruption.
- **Outcome:** A reliable digital skillset to use technology effectively, to locate and evaluate accurate information, and to discern scientifically and historically valid conclusions. **Skills / Topics:** Information literacy; scientific method; experimentation; evidence; correlation vs. causation.

These five outcomes are representative of a broad, cross-disciplinary skillset that some students acquire in school, though many do not. Like our best teachers, we can learn from the experiences of our most successful students. There are so many talented children across our schools who are brilliant and well-rounded, and they have harvested over many years deep intelligence and wide sensibilities, lest we forget that erudition is not a practical art. They have found a pathway that may be unique to them but must be afforded to others. Dewey describes this perfectly for us: "Education, the way I see it, is the gradual realization of self, of who we are, and what we stand for" (Dewey [1916] 2018).

Let that be our charge then: Recognizing the brilliance in all children and affirming that truth for all students across time. In his book, *Orbiting the Giant Hairball* (1998), creative thinker and artist Gordon MacKenzie relays a relevant story about his visits to elementary schools during his time working at Hallmark. He would ask students in the earliest grades how many artists there were in the room and nearly every hand shot up. When he asked the same question of students in third grade, a few would waive their arms. By sixth grade, only one or two students would slowly and sheepishly raise their hands. You see, without realizing it, adults at home and in school can methodically set the tone in defining for children what it is to "be normal." MacKenzie writes, "My guess is there was a time—perhaps when you were very young—when you had at least a fleeting notion of your own genius and were just waiting for some authority figure to come along and validate it for you. But none ever came."

5 Pioneering Leadership

Whenever you find yourself on the side of the majority, it is time to pause and reflect.

—*Mark Twain*

As with all battles worth winning, triumph demands courage. The answers we seek are often simple and obvious, and yet always daring. Across the education industry, we know many things that work well because our expertise, experience, and logic tell us so. Still, the hard truth is that district and state policies, legislative mandates, and industry trends prevent us from implementing them for fear of being wrong. It was not always this way, and it must not continue. Somewhere along the path to top-down management and state oversight, the system lost faith in our leaders and trust in our teachers. Systems of control tend to do that.

There is no doubt that bad ideas are often well-intentioned. The truth is, there was always a need for accountability, even standardization. There are too many schools and too much at stake to get things wrong. The lives and safety of children are too big a risk to allow free range for teachers and unchecked experimentation on instruction. Still, standardization means sameness and assimilation. State control over teacher licensure, methods, evaluation, and measurement has created a commonality among schools that borders on copy-and-paste, all in the name of high expectations.

Much of what we know about the onset of state-sponsored accountability was sold in good faith. There were many schools and districts that provided curriculum materials and quality controls that were lower and lesser, and children suffered (Ravitch 2002). In keeping with the themes of this text, it is important to note that high expectations for students is always the top priority in education. Accountability systems have normalized the use of standardized testing and data analysis, and that's not a bad thing. Some good has come from it, most importantly a focus on the performance of each and every child, and we cannot lose sight of that. Standardizing curriculum and instruction is another matter, and that has come at great cost. School districts have felt the push to purchase off-the-shelf curricula and not stray from it. Even more concerning are the strict appraisal systems and evaluation measures that are suffocating for teachers.

Standardized methods and monitoring tools have led to an understandable fear of repercussions for charting new paths, even those grounded in science. Of course, this is all frustrating for administrators and teacher-leaders who are doing their best to get it right and stay out of trouble. It is not unwise to say that a new experiment in literacy intervention or even teacher training could put students at risk. In fact, the premise of this text is that some things work better than others, and we should get those right first. Still, the goodwill that comes with studying reliable research and debating among colleagues what to try and what to wait on has been replaced by blogs and podcasts that do that for us. When this happens, what remains is not professional and collegial but regulatory and uniform. Mandates are clear, discussions are safe, and innovations are few.

The irony is so thick and obvious that it hardly needs mentioning. Though we preach innovation and change, the system has little tolerance for such things. Leaders across all levels are ready to applaud new ideas, but group consensus wins out and they never get off the ground. This paradox is apparent when we study the research on turnaround schools, where innovation is a prerequisite for improvement (Harbatkin 2024, 58–88). There is always a school that zigs when the others zag. In our most challenging schools, we often find a teacher or principal who invests in a new routine or tweaks an existing one and, as fate would have it, student achievement skyrockets. In these schools, innovation begets new solutions that research has not yet affirmed but will in time. The variations we find in the types of small group, push-in, and walk-to-intervention models are examples of creative solutions that have helped students learn and grow.

Innovations like these gain legs when leaders lift up what they believe to be right and then invest the time and training to do it well. This is not change for change sake. It is not random acts of instruction. It is not courageous in a "Let's try something out of the box and hope for the best" type of leadership, but in a "We're sticking to our beliefs and staying focused on these solutions" way of doing things. Courage of this sort requires the utmost credibility and confidence, which means we must have teachers and leaders who are experts on instructional best practice and unwavering about what works in schools. Courage as certainty. Courage as conviction.

Courage as Conviction

Across the education industry, we are conditioned more often than not to play things super-safe. Top-down management and accountability structures are unrelenting in telling us what to think and do and then installing consequences for not doing them. In many places, teachers and principals are so conditioned to follow research and policy that they no longer trust their guts because they don't have to. The brilliance of heroic teachers and principals is lost when we do such things, and we forsake our best people. Expecting teachers and administrators to follow a script has not moved our industry forward. It has already negatively impacted hiring and retention and silenced some of our best people.

The good news is that we can do something about it. This is part of the movie where confidence and conviction come in to save the day, for there has never been a substitute for knowing what you're talking about. It is a leadership superpower; it gives us the courage to leap tall buildings. PayPal co-founder and political activist Peter Thiel contends that those he works with are smart but cautious. Thiel says: "Brilliant thinking is rare, but courage is in even shorter supply than genius" (Thiel 2015, 23). In fact, when interviewing leaders for his own companies, he asks them: "Tell me something that's true that very few people agree with you on." Of course, many struggle to say something that doesn't sound like everyone else. As predicted, we get conditioned responses. We get groupthink. Alas, innovation has been marginalized, and stagnation institutionalized.

The education industry is not unlike most others. New ideas can be encouraged or not because someone smiles or rolls their eyes. In the current state of things, critics are ready to pounce on fresh ideas and social media pundits have already determined what is best practice. Many educators have taken sides on things like reading methods, classroom design, grading, and homework, and they rarely relent. This can mean one of two things: (i) That some are right and some are wrong. That while those on one side of an opinion are highly skilled and informed, those on the other side are sadly misguided or (ii) That the solutions are too complex and nuanced to be reduced to this versus that, and those who claim to know the most are just shouting the loudest.

A Quiet Confidence

There is a memorable moment in Super Bowl LIV where football legend Tom Brady is speaking with his teammates before the game and trying to calm their nerves. Of course, Brady has been through this before and he knows that his team is going to win because they are better prepared than their opponent. He tells the players: "We already know what they're going to do. We've got all the answers to the test. Now we just have to execute." In his opinion, they have the right plays to win the game and all they have to do now is perform them flawlessly. In a less famous example, a new elementary school principal was hired after many years as an administrator in high school. She was excited about her first day on the job and was certain that her organization of the end-of-day dismissal would go swimmingly, including the car line. She devised a new plan that she hoped and prayed would work, though she had no experience managing so many elementary school kids and their parents. As one could expect, dismissal that day was a disaster. She was well-intentioned but misinformed. She did not have the answers to the test. She was guessing.

In any organization, developing the knowledge and skillsets of leaders is paramount. In education, that means knowing the teacher's craft and what actions inside and outside of the classroom impact learning the most. The instructional levers provided in the previous chapters are great places to start. Most often, our best administrators were good teachers, and they have strong skillsets to draw from in coaching and training teachers and creating conditions in their schools where they can thrive. Those conditions range from clean and comfortable work environments to valuing teacher voice in school improvement decisions.

In school leadership, there are only two measurable outcomes. The first is safety, and the second is student achievement. Identifying the best teachers and leaders in any school district is as simple as figuring out who is positively impacting these outcomes. In fact, the research on best practices in education is centered on two distinct questions. Did this practice make students safer? Did this practice make students smarter? For purposes of this text, we have focused mostly on matters of achievement. Does student discussion make students smarter? Does writing make them smarter? Does quality teacher professional development make students smarter? Does effective small group intervention make them smarter? Of course, the answer to these four questions is "Yes." The trick then in school leadership development is making sure that those leaders who are making the most critical learning decisions are so credible in their understanding of best practices that they can be trusted to lead with little oversight. We need to know without hesitation that they are not guessing and then leave them alone.

The best principals across our communities have much to offer and, like our best teachers, they should be a primary source for professional development. Interestingly, highly effective principals and teachers are not always tapped to lead training or mentor others. As such, there remains a confounding reliance in school districts on think tanks and policy papers and less on learning from the school down the road. Make no mistake. In schools where real change is happening, learning must result. A powerful solution in one school might be high-functioning PLCs, but in another school it might be student data chats or study groups or a dozen other things. Whatever they decide, school leaders (including teacher-leaders) are not distracted by the next thing nor dissuaded by new things. They are not experimenting and then hoping it works. They are leading with conviction. They have the quiet confidence of knowing.

We can find this leadership characteristic identified across a wide range of disciplines and relevant research studies. It may be surprising to learn that Maslow wrote extensively on management and work culture throughout his storied career. His collection of journal entries on leadership was released under the title *Maslow on Management* (1998), and it has been reprinted and cited countless times. Maslow observed leaders across industries and saw a common trait among those who remained steadfast and focused while others were crippled by fear and anxiety that stopped them from acting: "It takes a certain kind of courage, which is simultaneously a kind of justified trust in ones' self and a justified trust in the goodness of the environment and of the future, to be able to face an unexpected, an unknown, unstructured situation without any guards or defenses, and with an innocent faith that one can improvise in the situation" (Maslow et al. 1998, 226).

In the context of schooling, the leaders who are most successful possess a deep knowledge base around cognition and learning that gives them faith that their decision-making will improve achievement (Grissom et al. 2021). While instructional expertise is foundational to effective school leadership, improvement in student outcomes results only when the leader can transfer that knowledge to teachers on the frontlines and filter out the mixed messages coming from state and district officials so the teachers can focus on doing what they do best.

Knowing Thy Enemy

Leadership that positively impacts outcomes requires the right balance between action and inaction. When we pull the right levers, things go well. When we pull all the levers at once, things go south. With so many initiatives in play and so much pressure to raise scores, leaders can make the mistake of tackling too many things. Worse than that, we might be spending a lot of time on initiatives that provide little return on learning. It may be tempting to reorganize the lunch lines or create new data systems that are certainly helpful in running a school but will not directly impact achievement. With each day bringing a new crisis, leaders can quickly lose sight of what matters most and turn their attention to things that are not the root causes of their downfall. With the stakes so high and the pressure mounting, we can blame the kids or the teachers or even the curriculum. Still, the true enemy is not teachers or parents, nor is it testing, policy, or process. Our only common enemy in education is "not learning." Yes, it is true, the hardest thing to defeat is the easiest one to locate.

If school leaders want to impact achievement, they must battle each day against "not learning." If learning occurs by design, then not learning does as well. Isolating the actions that will increase learning outcomes and identifying the barriers is step one. Any great plan for strategic improvement in schools must start there, and then not wiggle and waver. In their book *Strategy in Action*, Rachel Curtis and Elizabeth City (2015) provide great counsel and fair warning to leaders who jump on every proposal. "The result, paradoxically, is a strategic plan without a strategy. District staff work hard rather than smart, exhausting themselves with pockets of success and lots of wasted effort. Ultimately, students suffer" (Curtis and City 2015, 3).

Let's consider a middle school principal who is feeling the heat from the Superintendent to raise math scores that plummeted last year. The new principal has just come on board, and he is convinced that buying a new math computer program and hiring some high school kids to tutor his most struggling students are winning solutions. While those are creative approaches, the new principal doesn't realize that the problem is the core instruction and only in the seventh grade math classrooms. An analysis of the data shows that the two new teachers in that grade level have the lowest scores by far. The rest of the school's math team is strong. Though professional development, tutoring, and other things can continue, the school will not show improvement in math scores if someone does not help the two new teachers. More than that, the principal must resist the temptation to give up on his teachers because replacing new teachers with more new teachers is not going to get it done.

The solutions here are many-fold, and the principal has got to keep his attention there. He can still hold his staff meetings and cover lunch duty and attend the book fair, but he cannot let those things take his focus away from the students in those math classes. Without extending the example too far, let's also consider that some solutions are more likely to have immediate impact, some will take longer, and some are just window-dressing. Asking an assistant principal to visit the classrooms to monitor the instruction may be necessary but might not impact student performance at all. Assigning an instructional coach to mentor the teachers will certainly help but we may not see the impact on the scores for another year. It might be a better idea to have the teachers co-plan with a stronger teacher to impact the results this year, and for the students to receive extra help from push-in support or even walk-to-intervention if designed appropriately. None of these ideas are foolproof, but they get closer to the root cause and key metrics.

If we pull back just a little on the work of leading schools, we might see a clearer picture of what's happening below us. Students are interacting with new content and teachers are guiding them to mastery. Oh, and the clock is ticking. The school year is moving fast, and the circumstances do not change because the School Board just passed a new mandate, or the district tech team just scrapped the old data system for a new one. These changes may be necessary, but the time and energy required cannot impede learning today because today is not coming back. Some will say that the political forces are too strong to simply ignore other initiatives. Yes, it may be naïve to put a new policy or grant application or magnet program on the back burner, as long as we agree that it is equally naïve to think we are fixing things by taking on too many ideas, by jumping on every bandwagon, by doing many of them poorly, and by convincing ourselves that no one is noticing.

An investment in learning outcomes always comes with the discipline to stay focused. There are students who have missed too many days of school and who will not learn the content if we do not have a top-notch system in place for spiraled review. There are other students who understand the content fairly well, but who struggle to showcase their skills on tests so a weekly bell ringer activity on test literacy or error analysis is needed for those students to succeed. Only learning levers impact learning, and that may involve structures like questioning and discussion routines, checks for understanding, small group interventions, and reteaching. This is an important reminder that while some routines work better than others, nothing is full proof. The science of learning that many of us like to quote can only approximate the likely impact that some classroom actions may have. In the years after the release of his research on high-impact strategies, Marzano (2009) pointed out even the best strategies only work most of the time and only when they are done properly. "Since none are guaranteed to work, teachers must have the freedom and flexibility to adapt or try something different when student learning isn't forthcoming" (Marzano 2009, 30–7).

Having certainty about what works in classrooms comes only through experience, not from a YouTube video. This is a cautionary tale for teachers and leaders who are quick to jump on trends without fully knowing the context. Yes, we have all made this mistake. The evolving trends around best practices are found in every school system. We know that a longer school day or extended school year would benefit many learners, but we rarely implement such things. We know that explicit skill-building (math fluency, for example) is critical to student success, but we find some schools back away for fear that more "drill and kill" worksheets may result. We know that students who don't read well need more time to read, but we have shifted away from independent reading time and even reading practice at home because it has been implemented poorly so many times. Homework can be helpful to student achievement, but we have moved away from it because it can be inequitable and a waste of time if done poorly. This kind of back and forth regarding best practice goes on and on in education, and many educators subscribe to the current narrative even when they know that there's a better way.

Trusting the Experts: Teachers and Kids

The more time we invest in observing and learning from the best teachers in our profession, the simpler it becomes to tackle this complex thing we call "educating all children." In listening closely to teachers and students, they remind us over and over again that the most overlooked practice is not really a practice at all. It's a belief system: Setting high expectations. There is simply no research anywhere, nor any practical reality, that asserts that there are some kids who can learn while others cannot.

Though variables like poverty negatively impact learning, it is not poverty that makes children underachieve. It is the expectations we place on them that undermines their performance, among many other prejudices in play. As author and educator, Ken Robinson said it: "Circumstances are not destiny" (Robinson 2015, 24). The teachers who work in our most challenging schools have taught us how much expectations matter, as well as the structures for raising the bar for kids. We don't have to look any further for evidence of what works than this shrewd comment from a fifth grade student: "I like this class because it makes me feel smart."

The levers presented in this text are provided to help students feel smart, and they are formed from the feedback of the experts who know best. If we stay true to the long history of teaching as a proud vocation, we know that students cannot feel smart if we haven't created the classroom conditions for becoming smart, including challenging coursework, higher-order questioning, teacher modeling and think aloud, discussion and debate, feedback and praise, and time on task. It is not professional nor prudent to let colleagues, parents, or kids talk us down from high expectations. A poignant example is found in this comment from a teacher who was counseling a student through hard times. "Yes, I understand that your socks are dirty. But just because you have dirty socks doesn't mean you can't learn."

Our teachers and students have taught us that raising expectations requires us to act on those beliefs, to be bold in our decisions, resolute in our convictions, and devout in our studies. Strangely, knowing more gives us permission to do less. In fact, an important step in school improvement is one that is hard for school and district leaders to say out loud. We need to do less and do it well. This will require a change in mindsets, as we are so entrenched in the bureaucracy of schooling that it is hard to imagine another way.

The constant drum of continuous improvement has compelled schools and districts to try everything they can to improve scores, to write it all down in strategic plan after strategic plan, to invent measures we never had before, and to assign department heads to monitor our maze of solutions. From high above, the maze appears connected, even symmetrical. While inside the maze, it is hard to see what is around the next corner, and it is easy to get lost, turned around, and convinced that there is no way out. As public servants, we have contributed to this mess. In our rush to fix all things, educators take on too many solutions in a chaotic attempt to leave no idea unspoken and no innovation untried. Whatever we decide, we will not ignite the next generation of schools as centers of confidence and creativity by simply stoking the same-old bureaucracy.

People over Policy

The path forward for leaders and managers of any organization is the same one available to those of us in education: Investing in our people. Agency and voice. Interconnectedness. Common understanding. Kindness and respect. This might be best described as the ecology of people. The changing landscape of schools will require that we hire and keep the best people we have, or risk losing them to online platforms and other industries. Across the wide landscape of corporations, non-profits, political action groups, and civic organizations, young professionals crave structures that are *people-centered* and industries that are *purpose seeking*. We must build school systems that involve people and serve people, because that is the business we are in. Not only is this the right way to lead, but it also advances our agenda for achievement. Yes, our outcomes will be advanced by systems that are participatory.

If any system can embrace collaboration and collegiality as central to its organizational structure, it is education. We are a system of teachers, including those working as school administrators and central office executives. If teachers cannot build such a system, no one can. Top-down management in education has not worked, and new structures must be built to support the kind of schools we envision. This new way of doing things will require us to pull together our students, parents, teachers, and community leaders in a way that is much more organic and less institutional than what we have now. Teachers and students will be much more involved in leading the changes in their schools, and they will form their own niches that are self-organized in support of their personal growth and advancement.

We can improve our systems by designing departments and actions that are aligned to each other and to common values that connect people and practices. In turn, these systems will promote more desirable schools and workplaces that are focused on human conditions, not bureaucratic ones.

This kind of change requires leaders who are confident enough to lead others to action. We have plenty of leaders in education who have modeled this for us, and the results are extraordinary and lasting.

Whether we embrace it or not, the future will require a more soulful educational experience for our students that will not feel contrived and cookie-cutter in having everybody follow the same bell schedule and complete the same assignments. If these changes do not occur, public schools could become the second choice (or last choice) of parents in the competitive market of schooling. In fact, the trends are already evident. If we are unable or unwilling to innovate, public schools will continue to exist but will be less relevant in the marketplace.

In response, our industry must invest in developing and promoting leaders who have great expertise and deep conviction, those with strong core beliefs and who live out those beliefs through word and deed. Confident and humble. Approachable and authentic. The future will demand that our leaders, like our systems, remain nimble and forward-thinking, always ready to take us to places we have never been before. Like any emerging idea, this one will require pioneering leadership.

Courage as Creativity

The next generation will bring great pressures upon public schools to rebrand and repurpose their work. This will require leaders who can see around the bend, and who are comfortable as co-learners and co-innovators alongside their teachers. In fact, it may be true that teachers will lead schools in the future via academic deans or some sort of teacher council. We will still need great principals, but their work will shift from managers of people and policies to thought partners and facilitators of teacher and student innovation. Yes, school operations will remain critical to student safety and success, and someone will do that work. It just won't be the principal.

These changes may sound daring to some, but it is hard to imagine creative and confident kids emerging from any system that is tired and uninspiring. Yes, schools and school districts must be self-actualized as well. The system cannot set goals to get all students to graduate or read at grade level and yet have conditions that would make that unlikely. The system cannot establish a vision around improved professionalism and collegiality and then create structures that are more isolating than collaborative.

In turning back to Maslow, he developed what was known as normative or ideal social psychology. In essence, he subscribed to the science of possibilities. In effect, he sought to uncover the culture that would be generated by one thousand self-actualizing people on some sheltered island where they would not be interfered with (Maslow et al. 1998). In keeping with his fascination for such things, he observed successful people and wrote down what he saw. He was interested in true leadership, in actual game-changers. If Maslow were here, he would tell us that he wasn't much for those who only talked a good game. "That's the way you tell the difference between fruitfulness and sterility, between talkers and doers, between people who change the world and people who are helpless in it" (Maslow et al. 1998, 5).

As leaders, we cannot shrink from the challenge of creativity and enterprise. The solutions we seek are literally right in front of us if we dare to act on them. Yes, it is easier to stay in the moment and survive the day, and who would blame us with so much on our plates? The forces at work to keep things stable have legitimate reasons for their resistance, and time is one of them. Fear of failure is another. A way forward may be implementing only one system change that tilts the current trajectory just a little. The following innovations are provided as places to begin, as well as a challenge of sorts to evolve our system faster and overcome the numbness that comes from sitting still too long.

Shifting Priorities / School Improvement Loops to Consider

The following practices are provided as proof of concept for leaders as they are forged from observations of great schools in action. They are provided as approaches to strategic planning for leaders who wish to narrow their focus and impact outcomes. These solutions should not be viewed as independent variables to school improvement, but as co-dependent and mutually assured. Each one of the solutions below posits the notion that core beliefs drive core actions unless someone chickens out along the way, and that the reverse is also true.

- **Teacher Growth and Leadership:** Schools that retain great teachers will win the day. The research on teacher effectiveness is clear and decisive. There is nothing that matters more to student achievement than great instruction. Successful school leaders build great teams, beginning with hiring the right people. For this reason, the hiring process is tightly managed to ensure that only the best candidates are selected. The most effective leaders are fully invested in these decisions, and do not assign them to others to complete. Celebrating new and veteran teachers is central to building a positive work culture. Teamwork should be evident across all meetings, trainings, and events. In the most successful schools, distributed leadership is shaped and promoted. Teachers are trusted to lead major initiatives, including professional development. Teacher voice in decision-making is encouraged and valued. Sustainable student achievement is only possible in schools where staff retention is strong and teacher agency is cultivated.

- **Acceleration over Remediation:** Student expectations are built by design. Master schedules, teaching assignments, and tutoring support are just some examples of the decisions school leaders must consider when creating the right learning environment for students. Though remediation is necessary, practice and proficiency in grade-level coursework is the goal. While schools should always celebrate student progress, progress is not an outcome. The most successful schools build actionable, verifiable systems of acceleration designed to get all students to mastery. This begins with a belief in high expectations and leads to a culture of high achievement. These schools put their vision for excellence into the practices of ambitious instruction. This includes a relentless focus on key instructional levers and routines.
- **Strategic Restraint:** Successful leaders learn quickly that less is more. The most successful schools are strategic and purposeful in narrowing their focus to a few key actions that impact student performance. These schools build structures based on a core belief that doing a few things well is more effective than doing many things poorly. Schools can be overwhelmed by a constant flow of data, information, and ideas coming at them from social media posts, educational conferences, research studies, and a long line of instructional experts. Successful leaders are skillful in absorbing and filtering information to keep themselves and their school teams focused. Some strategic actions are adopted and cultivated while others are rejected or delayed because they might distract from organizational culture or outcomes. In these schools, student achievement is positively impacted not by a specific strategy

or process that a school selects but from a singular belief and resolve in doing these things well on behalf of students.

- **Data Agency and Agility:** Data can inform and empower learning, or it cannot. The most successful schools collect the right types and amounts of data with the singular mission of getting all students to meet grade-level standards. These schools also provide ready access to the data to teachers, students, and families. A key element in successful schools is not only access but agency. The use of data to inform teacher decision-making and improve student self-reliance is key. Data outcomes are less likely to improve achievement if students are not responding to the data with an actionable method for improving their own performance. Schools must remain agile as the school year progresses so they are ready to respond at any moment. This might mean changing student interventions or even shifting teaching assignments. The decisions must be collaborative and logical, not simply reactionary. Success in schools is not derived from reviewing the data but from a well-executed plan for reshaping it. In this manner, schools know what students need to reach mastery without fail and without guesswork.
- **Shared Accountability:** Successful schools have high professional standards. The curriculum, instruction, and interventions are skillfully designed and effectively monitored. Leaders in these schools are well-versed in effective classroom processes and pedagogy. Instructional time is creatively planned and closely protected. Leaders know that student achievement for all is not possible if quality instruction is only available to some. Successful schools do not require top-down management or government mandates to hold them accountable. These schools create a culture of their own based on shared purpose and trust, beginning with a commitment among staff to learn and grow their craft. Staff members hold each other accountable in a collegial and supportive manner. Classroom observations and feedback are constructive and affirming. In these schools, no student goes unnoticed. Absences are addressed as nothing is more detrimental than lost instructional time. Staff absences are anticipated and strategic solutions are predetermined so learning is not interrupted. In the most successful schools, personal and professional relationships are evident and celebrating a student or colleague never gets old.

Shifting Mindsets / System Changes to Consider

The following system shifts may be necessary in devising the kinds of learning experiences and outcomes we seek. They are provided as possible entry points for leaders who are looking for either subtle jabs at the system or powerful gut punches to dramatically reform and disrupt the norm. None of these innovations alone will upend the system, and some are already in the works across schools and districts. Still, implementing some of these solutions may go a long way in sending messages about changing priorities and informing the system that we are not just about talk, but action.

- **Professionalism / Self-Governance:** The education industry must come to grips with the shortcomings of its professional development, credentialing, and appraisal models. None of them work well enough at present to get us where we need to be. Whatever they become, our solutions must involve higher degrees of professionalism and self-governance on behalf of teachers. Though it is incumbent upon the industry to identify and support struggling teachers, the time and energy spent on our current appraisal systems cannot be sustained. The same degree of voice, choice, and ownership of learning that we wish for our students must be afforded to our teachers. If done well, this will raise the stakes on instruction, not lower them. It will put pressure on the teaching profession to invest in high-fidelity models by which rich instruction becomes the norm and poor instruction is rooted out.
- **Curriculum Shifts / Workplace Skills:** We are never going to inspire, engage, and motivate children if they view their subjects and lessons as disconnected or even random. We must identify the key skills and concepts that students must master and then ensure that we have viable, relatable curriculum materials that cross subject areas. This includes cross-training among teachers of various grades and subjects. A key readiness measure for students is their ability to communicate effectively, solve complex problems, think creatively, innovate, pitch their ideas to others, and accept critical feedback. We must find ways to intentionally integrate these skills into our lessons. Some content knowledge (names, dates, places) will be replaced by soft skills like navigating our communities and workplaces, building authentic relationships, and developing our personal brands.

- **Flexible Scheduling / Inductive Learning:** Schools must be designed around each student's needs, including flexible school days and alternative learning environments. There will be very little room in the future for cookie-cutter lessons and assignments. Learning will become greatly inductive, place-based, and personal. Assessment will be wide and deep, from informal talks to juried presentations. While rigorous classroom instruction remains first and foremost, we will provide students with time and space for personal reflection, peer interaction, and independent research. In fact, the day may come where we provide students a day off campus (perhaps at a local college, museum, or business) learning in different environments, researching topics of their own choosing, and developing original business ventures.
- **Learning Outside / Field Experiences:** The future of learning may someday lead to deeper, richer curriculum threads that connect lessons to student lives, passions, and ambitions. This may lead to scheduled "breaks" from school where students have the time to take part in their own research activities or longitudinal projects that go far beyond canned research papers. This may include career exploration activities at local tech companies or short stints as docents at local museums. Of course, this is not to suggest that these longer breaks from school will occur at home unsupervised. Such opportunities could be supervised off campus with greater participation from our community partners or through planned teacher sabbaticals.
- **Volunteerism / Activism:** The future of schools will certainly be connected to the promising practices occurring now in revitalizing our neighborhoods and building sustainable communities. This will require our schools and communities to collaborate in giving students purposeful opportunities to volunteer and support their neighbors. These partnerships can provide students with rich lessons in self-respect, empathy, and pride through positive community activism. A rich, meaningful brand of volunteerism will go a long way in helping our young people view community involvement as something they *want* to do and *should* do and not as something they are *compelled* to do as a means of accumulating the community service hours required for school clubs or scholarship applications.

If we do this well, the entire experience of schooling will feel more meaningful and personal for students, from the relationships they form to the assignments they complete. What students learn and how they learn will make sense to them, and they will want to learn more. Creating such schools will require us to build systems and processes from the student outward. From the curriculum outward. From the lessons outward. From the core. And our best teachers are the ones who know best how to do it.

A great number of things we have built must be reshaped, beginning with assessment and data systems. Creative and confident kids do not evolve from statistical methods and measures like grade point averages and percentile ranks. The industry may still capture these data, but they are not sufficient in describing student knowledge and abilities. Children are distinctive and expressive human beings, not data points. The same is true for teachers, who routinely navigate similar rank-order metrics that are intended to define effectiveness. This is yet another top-down solution that is inefficient and ineffective in improving teacher practice. We already hear the frustrations from students and teachers, and a rebellion is mounting. *My worth and value are unique and complex. I will not be reduced to a number.*

These system changes are consistent with the recurring themes of this text in building self-confidence and self-esteem, and much of what has been said of children and their development over time is true for adults. If we are valued and supported, we grow in confidence and feel empowered that "I/we can accomplish anything." The opposite of this is not pessimism or discouragement but something even worse. It is called "learned helplessness," the damning realization that "I cannot do this. I am not smart. I cannot learn. In fact, I am not even going to try." If we are not careful, teachers can fall into similar patterns.

Whether we are ready or not, our students, parents, and teachers will demand to be heard, to have a seat at the table, and they are not wrong. They will demand immediate access to decision-making, and more control over curriculum and timelines. They will expect a system that makes each child's path unique within learning encounters that are dynamic and diverse. Of course, this is incredibly difficult for current managers to conceive of since most grew up in an age of assembly lines and top-down corporate hierarchies. In the same way, districts struggle to imagine solutions outside the current accountability measures, appraisal frameworks, and school bell schedules. We are so deeply conditioned and bound by such things that our minds cannot easily unravel them. Making this work will not come without predictable resistance and egregious missteps. We may find our efforts hindered because connections and relationships are lacking. We may find a lack of understanding and trust, not only in leadership but in the system. Whatever forces we encounter, we can overcome them in large part by upending them. If we get it right, leaders can spin the solutions so forcefully that no energy is lost and everyone is hanging on with both hands and enjoying the ride.

Pioneer Species—The Consequence of Leadership

In making this new reality a reality we should be clear that there is much at stake in whatever we decide. If we remain resolute, the ideas presented in this text are very much doable. Change will require persistence, but no miracles are required. Leaders do not need to overreach, but they do need to focus and start somewhere. Success will be evident when classroom routines are established, learning levers are codified into practice, and teacher leadership is behind it.

Yes, we can afford to move slowly because moving fast will not work. It is true that all systems must evolve to avoid extinction; no one is predicting a day when public schools no longer exist. It's actually worse than that. If we do not evolve, we may see a day when the marketplace shifts and public schools become less relevant (maybe irrelevant), less appreciated (maybe unappreciated), less inspiring (maybe uninspiring), and less necessary (maybe unnecessary). The only antidote is leadership.

Leaders have always had the capacity to change the course of history, and we tend to act faster when we are most threatened. In keeping with this theme, let's turn our attention to fascinating science known as "ecological succession." In short, this is the change process that an ecological community (like a swamp or forest) goes through over time. To picture this, try to imagine the expansive wilderness of the Northwest, maybe somewhere in the far reaches of Montana. A small, isolated community of plants grows over time (through thousands of years) into a complex, self-governing, vibrant ecological community. This community may continue, seemingly unchanged, for generations (like a school system, for instance)—until something happens. It can be a small disturbance or a catastrophic event. In our example, this could be a fire or a landslide or a new species. In any case, something happens. In fact, something always happens. It is inevitable.

What comes next matters most. The first brave species to emerge after that change event, even after the most catastrophic events, are called "pioneer species." These new species are different somehow, hardy and bold and ready to start anew. They don't wait around. They move in and colonize the damaged ecosystem, the first step in a continuum of ecological succession that leads to an even stronger and more diverse ecosystem. Think of it as the benefit to the system for being brave enough to start anew, as a return on leadership. In fact, we might define this as the "consequence of leadership," one's responsibility to alter their own environment and provide a subtle disturbance that forces a change that will result in a stronger, more stable, and more diverse system.

In the process of ecological succession, new life forms in places that were formally barren. One such stage is called primary succession, the establishment of new habitats where there were none previously (going where no habitat has gone before). The other stage is called secondary succession, the regeneration of life for a community that has been reshaped following one of these change events (a vibrant, new habitat that is stronger than the one before).

This new life formed through ecological succession evolves from a few pioneering species into a climax community of increased diversity and mass that, in turn, provides a greater resistance to invasive species in the future. The system is more mature than it was before, better equipped to take on future changes, and ready to maximize all the resources at its disposal. The system is stronger than ever, confident, nimble, and quicker to react to and recover from the inevitable forces that are out to destroy it. Let us endeavor to unearth such a system for the betterment of our schools and children. Stronger than ever. Confident and nimble.

All we need now are a few pioneering leaders and some rich damn soil.

Afterword: An Open Letter to Students

Dear students: No matter the degree of struggle and depth of sadness that you face in your life, there are many who stand in testimony before you in saying that better days lay ahead. The pangs of youth can bring so much heartache that it is a wonder how any of us survive it. The hard realities of poverty and trauma, the gripping tensions of crooked smiles and strained relationships, and the gross amalgam of mixed messages from parents, teachers, and online influences leave you struggling to sort it all out. No matter what you hear, trust me on this one. There is a place for you in this world.

When I was a child, I survived a great many struggles that stole my confidence and convinced me that I was not smart, nor privileged, nor special. After many years of questioning my worth and future, I discovered something that I want you to know. That the other people out there were no smarter or deserving than I was, and they are no smarter or deserving than you. Though this may seem obvious coming from a teacher, I promise you that learning, hard work, and resilience are key ingredients to finding your way out and securing some peace.

Of course, the truth is that you cannot just wake up one day and expect to be brilliant and successful. You see, confidence is not given. It is earned. And so it is that being successful requires action, not luck. With that in mind, it is time to get busy at getting better, and here are two actions that will serve you well:

Be curious. Successful people are curious beings. Formal education, like going to college, is not what separates the most successful people from those who are not. In fact, some of the wisest people you will meet never went to college, and there are many others who obtained their degrees and don't know much at all. They don't tell you that in school. So, a first step is taking pride in yourself by taking pride in your own learning, in knowing a little bit about a great many things. Not because knowing things is an outward display of intelligence, but because knowing things is an inward display of curiosity and confidence. And people always find that appealing. While you may be interested at this point in sports or dance or music, start learning more about those things and you will soon unravel threads that lead to new topics to learn about. You see, curiosity is exponential.

Be resourceful. Successful people are rarely lucky. Despite what we see on social media, most people don't hit the lottery. Most really do earn their success by standing out in some way, usually through a combination of hard work, hustle, and creative ambition. What you may not realize is that your reputation is being formed right now and how people perceive you matters a great deal in life. Whether you are working the register at a fast-food joint, picking up equipment after practice, or stacking chairs after a youth group meeting, do it well. Don't shortcut it. Don't do things sloppy in five minutes that you can do perfectly in ten minutes. Yes, even when no one is around.

Along the way, explore your passions across many topics, from faith to politics. Test out new ideas of your own, and don't trust someone else's take as being true or even inspired. Shakespeare warned us about that. If you do this right, a world of interesting things will appear before you, and doing something special with your life will make itself known. Of course, none of this will happen quickly so be patient a bit longer. You are still young, and sometimes you must listen and endure a bit while others prattle on about how much smarter or prettier they are than you.

Stay true to yourself because, you see, goodness does win out most of the time. There really are happy endings, even if the bad moments never leave us. Across an abundant and meaningful life, we all must learn that struggle and toil come first and then victories later. And trust me in saying that humility comes before honor and honor before triumph. It is the kind of stuff you believed long ago, when you thought the world was right and good. In his book *All I Really Need to Know I Learned in Kindergarten,* Robert Fulghum writes: "I believe that imagination is stronger than knowledge. That myth is more potent than history. That dreams are more powerful than facts. That hope always triumphs over experience. That laughter is the only cure for grief. And I believe that love is stronger than death."

Trust me, life has a way of evening the score. So be strong and keep your eyes straight ahead. Try your best to tune out the ugly clang of prejudice, the unsettling drum of superiority, and the cynical sneers that come your way.

And know this. Though you are blind and cannot see, there is a place for each of us in the offering. You will somehow escape the treachery. You will somehow reap your reward. You will walk in the sun. And you will be free.

References

Aristotle. *Metaphysics*.1.2.982.

Carpenter, Shana, Steven Pan, and Andrew Butler. 2022. "The Science of Effective Learning with Spacing and Retrieval Practice." *Nature Reviews Psychology* 1, 496–511. https://doi.org/10.1038/s44159-022-00089-1.

Curtis, Rachel, and Elizabeth City. 2015. *Strategy in Action: How School Systems Can Support Powerful Teaching and Learning*. Havard Education Press.

Dehaene, S. 2020. *How We Learn: The New Science of Education and the Brain*. Penguin.

Dewey, John. [1916] 2018. *Democracy and Education*. Myers Education Press.

Dewey, John. [1938] 2015. *Education and Experience*. Simon and Schuster.

Ebbinghaus, Hermann. [1885] 1913. "Memory (ha ruger & ce bussenius, trans.)." *New York: Teachers College*. 39.

Fulghum, Robert. 2004. *All I Really Need to Know I Learned in Kindergarten*. Ballantine Books.

Furlong, Michael, Douglas Smith, Tina Springer, and Erin Dowdy. 2021. "Bored with School! Bored with Life? Well-Being Characteristics Associated with a School Boredom Mindset." *Journal of Positive School Psychology* 5 (1): 1–21.

Goleman, Daniel. 1995. *Emotional Intelligence: Why It Can Matter More Than IQ*. Bantam Books.

Good, H. G. 1962. *A History of American Education*. Macmillan.

Grissom, Jason A., Anna J. Egalite, and Constance A. Lindsay. 2021. "How Principals Affect Students and Schools: A Systematic Synthesis of Two Decades of Research." The Wallace Foundation. http://www.wallacefoundation.org/ principalsynthesis. https://doi.org/10.59656/EL-SB1065.001.

Hanushek, Eric A., and Margaret E. Raymond. 2005. "Does School Accountability Lead to Improved Student Performance?" *Journal of Policy Analysis and Management: The Journal of the Association for Public Policy Analysis and Management* 24 (2): 297–327.

Harbatkin, Erica, Lam Pham, Christoper Redding, and Alex Moran. 2024. "What Are the Side Effects of School Turnaround? A Systematic Review." *Review of Research in Education* 48 (1): 58–88.

Hattie, John. 2009. *Visible Learning: A Synthesis of over 800 Meta-Analyses Relating to Achievement*. Routledge.

Hattie, John. 2017. "Hattie: Collective Efficacy." Interview by James Nottingham. *The Learning Pit*. https://vimeo.com/267382804.

Kliebard, Herbert. 2004. *The Struggle for the American Curriculum – 1893–1958*. RoutledgeFalmer.

Ladson-Billings, Gloria. 2022. "What Should Culturally Relevant Teaching Look Like Today? Gloria Ladson-Billings Explains." Interview by Madeline Will and Ileana Najarro. *Education Week*. https://www.edweek.org/leadership/what-should-culturally-relevant-teaching-look-like-today-gloria-ladson-billings-explains/2022/04.

Lewis, C.S. 1952. *The World's Last Night and Other Essays*. Harcourt Brace & Company.

MacKenzie, Gordon. 1998. *Orbiting the Giant Hairball: A Corporate Fool's Guide to Surviving with Grace*. Penguin Publishing.

Marzano, Robert. 2009. "Setting the Record Straight on 'High Yield' Strategies.'" *Phi Delta Kappan* 91 (6): 30–7.

Marzano, Robert, and Debra Pickering. 2010. *The Highly Engaged Classroom*. Solution Tree.

Marzano, Robert, Debra Pickering, and Jane Pollock. 2001. *Classroom Instruction That Works: Research-Based Strategies for Increasing Student Achievement*. Association for Supervision and Curriculum Development.

Maslow, Abraham, Deborah Stephens, and Gary Heil. 1998. *Maslow on Management*. John Wiley.

Muijs, Daniel. 2021. "Rosenshine and Why Teacher Effectiveness Research Still Makes Sense but Isn't the Full Story." *Education Ruminations*. June 11, 2021. https://educationruminations.com.

Ordofa, Begna, and Amare Asgedom. 2022. "School Accountability and Its Relationship with Learning Outcomes: A Systematic Literature Review." *Social Sciences & Humanities Open* 6 (1): 100358.

Orth, U., and R. W Robins. 2022. "Is High Self-Esteem Beneficial? Revisiting a Classic Question." *American Psychologist* 77 (1): 5–17. https://doi.org/10.1037/amp0000922.

Opper, Isaac. 2019. "How Teacher Effectiveness Spills over into Other Classrooms. Research Brief." *Rand Corporation*. https://www.rand.org/pubs/research_briefs/RB10066.html.

Ravitch, Diana. 2002. "A Brief History of Testing and Accountability." *Hoover Digest*. https://www.hoover.org/research/brief-history-testing-and-accountability.

Reynolds, D., P. Sammons, B. De Fraine, J. Van Damme, T. Townsend, C. Teddlie, and S. Stringfield. 2014. "Educational Effectiveness Research (EER): A State-of-the-Art Review." *School Effectiveness and School Improvement* 25 (2): 197–230.

Robins, Richard, Jessica Tracy, Kali Trzesniewski, Jeff Potter, and Samuel Gosling. 2001. "Personality Correlates of Self-Esteem." *Journal of Research in Personality* 35 (4): 463–82.

Robinson, Ken. 2015. *Creative Schools: The Grassroots Revolution That's Transforming Education*. Viking.

Rosenshine, Barak, Meister, Carla, and Chapman, Saul. 1996. "Teaching Students to Generate Questions: A Review of the Intervention Studies." *Review of Educational Research* 66 (2): 181–221.

Rosenshine, Barak. 2012. "Principles of Instruction. Research-Based Strategies That All Teachers Should Know." *American Educator* Spring 2012: 12–19.

Sanders, W. L., and Rivers, J. C. 1996. *Cumulative and Residual Effects of Teachers on Future Student Academic Achievement* (Research Progress Report). Knoxville, TN: University of Tennessee, Value-Added Research and Assessment Center.

Scriven, Michael. 2002. "The Limits of Explication." *Argumentation* 16 (1): 47–57.

Thiel, Peter. 2015. *Zero to One: Notes on Startups, or How to Build the Future*. Random House.

Willingham, D. 2010. *Why Don't Students Like School?* Jossey-Bass.

Zahn, Lexia, Guo, Dingrong, Chen, Gang, and Jiongjoing Yang. 2018. "Effects of Repetition Learning on Associative Recognition over Time: Role of the Hippocampus and Prefrontal Cortex." *Cognitive Science* 12: 1–14.

About the Author

Daniel J. Evans has led an accomplished career as a teacher and leader and is a sought-after speaker and trainer on educational reform. Dan stared down his own childhood struggles and turned despair and defeat into a lifetime of success through faith and love for children and teachers. He is a former *Principal of the Year* and Chief Academic Officer. His expertise in literacy best practices and high-yield instructional strategies drives his passion for what works in schools. His first book *The Instructional Soul: Leading Schools with a Spirit of Innovation* debuted in 2019. Dan most recently served as the Chief Academic Officer for one of the nation's largest public school districts. During his tenure, the district earned its highest achievement scores in reading, math, and science in its history. He is a former English teacher, high school principal, and district research and assessment lead. He is currently an adjunct professor, as well as a mentor to teachers and leaders. He can be reached via his website: danevansauthor.com.